RETHINKING INDIA SERIES

THE MINORITY CONUNDRUM
LIVING IN MAJORITARIAN TIMES

EDITED BY
TANWEER FAZAL

VINTAGE
An imprint of Penguin Random House

VINTAGE

USA | Canada | UK | Ireland | Australia
New Zealand | India | South Africa | China

Vintage is part of the Penguin Random House group of companies
whose addresses can be found at global.penguinrandomhouse.com

Published by Penguin Random House India Pvt. Ltd
7th Floor, Infinity Tower C, DLF Cyber City,
Gurgaon 122 002, Haryana, India

First published in Vintage by Penguin Random House India 2020

10 9 8 7 6 5 4 3 2 1

The book is a collection of essays of the respective authors who have exercised
reasonable diligence to ensure veracity of the content and is by no means intended
to hurt or offend any segment of persons.

The views and opinions expressed in this book are the authors' own and the facts
are as reported by them which have been verified to the extent possible, and the
publishers are not in any way liable for the same.

ISBN 9780670092956

Typeset in Bembo Std by Manipal Technologies Limited, Manipal
Printed at Replika Press Pvt. Ltd, India

www.penguin.co.in

Contents

Series Editors' Note

Psychologists tell us that the only *true* enemies we have are the faces looking back at us in the mirror. Today, we in India need to take a long, hard look at ourselves in the mirror. With either actual or looming crises in every branch of government, at every level, be it centre, state or local; with nearly every institution failing; with unemployment at historically high rates; with an ecosystem ready to implode; with a healthcare system in shambles; with an education system on the brink of collapse; with gender, caste and class inequities unabating; with civil society increasingly characterized by exclusion, intolerance and violence; with our own minorities living in fear; our hundreds of millions of fellow citizens in penury; and with few prospects for the innumerable youth of this nation in the face of all these increasingly intractable problems, the reflection is not sightly. Our true enemies are not external to us, not Pakistani terrorists or Bangladeshi migrants, but our own selves: our own lack of imagination, communication, cooperation and dedication towards achieving the India of our destiny and dreams.

Our Constitution, as the preamble so eloquently attests, was founded upon the fundamental values of the dignity of the individual and the unity of the nation, envisioned in relation to a radically egalitarian justice. These bedrock ideas, though perhaps especially pioneered by the likes of Jawaharlal Nehru, B.R. Ambedkar, M.K. Gandhi, Maulana Azad, Sardar Patel, Sarojini Naidu, Jagjivan Ram, R. Amrit Kaur, Rammanohar Lohia and others, had emerged as a broad consensus among the many founders of this nation, cutting across divergent social and political ideologies. Giving shape to that vision, the architects of modern India strived to ensure that each one of us is accorded equal opportunities to live with dignity and security, has equitable access to a better life, and is an equal partner in this nation's growth.

Yet, today we find these most basic constitutional principles under attack. Nearly all the public institutions that were originally created in order to fight against dominance and subservience are in the process of subversion, creating new hierarchies instead of dismantling them, generating inequities instead of ameliorating them. Government policy merely pays lip service to egalitarian considerations, while the actual administration of 'justice' and implementation of laws are in fact perpetuating precisely the opposite: illegality, criminality, corruption, bias, nepotism and injustice of every conceivable stripe. And the rapid rise of social intolerance and manifold exclusions (along the lines of gender, caste, religion, etc.) effectively whittle down and even sabotage an inclusive conception of citizenship, polity and nation.

In spite of these and all the other unmentioned but equally serious challenges posed at this moment, there are in fact new sites for sociopolitical assertion re-emerging. There are new calls arising for the reinstatement of the letter and spirit of our Constitution, not just *normatively* (where we battle things out ideologically) but also *practically* (the battle at the level of policy articulation and implementation). These calls are not simply partisan, nor are they exclusionary or zero-sum. They witness the wide participation of youth, women, the historically disadvantaged in the process of finding a new voice, minorities, members of majority communities, and progressive individuals all joining hands in solidarity.

We at the Samruddha Bharat Foundation proudly count ourselves among them. The Foundation's very raison d'être has been to take serious cognizance of India's present and future challenges, and to rise to them. Over the past two years, we have constituted numerous working groups to critically rethink social, economic and political paradigms to encourage a transformative spirit in India's polity. Over 400 of India's foremost academics, activists, professionals and policymakers across party lines have constructively engaged in this process. We have organized and assembled inputs from *jan sunwai*s (public hearings) and *jan manch*s (public platforms) that we conducted across several states, and discussed and debated these ideas with leaders of fourteen progressive political parties, in an effort to set benchmarks for a future common minimum programme. The overarching idea has been to try to breathe new life and spirit into the cold and self-serving logic of political and administrative processes, linking them to and informing them by grass-roots realities, fact-based research and social experience, and actionable social-scientific knowledge. And to do all of this with harmony and heart, with sincere emotion and national feeling.

In order to further disseminate these ideas, both to kick-start a national dialogue and to further build a consensus on them, we are bringing out this set of fourteen volumes highlighting innovative ideas that seek to deepen and further the promise of India. This is not an academic exercise; we do not merely spotlight structural problems, but also propose disruptive solutions to each of the pressing challenges that we collectively face. All the essays, though authored by top academics, technocrats, activists, intellectuals and so on, have been written purposively to be accessible to a general audience, whose creative imagination we aim to spark and whose critical feedback we intend to harness, leveraging it to further our common goals.

The inaugural volume has been specifically dedicated to our norms, to serve as a fresh reminder of our shared and shareable overlapping values and principles, collective heritage and resources. Titled *Vision for a Nation: Paths and Perspectives*, it champions a plural, inclusive, just, equitable and prosperous India, and is committed to individual dignity, which is the foundation of the unity and vibrancy of the nation.

The thirteen volumes that follow turn from the normative to the concrete. From addressing the problems faced by diverse communities—Adivasis, Dalit-Bahujans, Other Backward Classes (OBCs)—as well as women and minorities, to articulating the challenges that we face with respect to jobs and unemployment, urbanization, healthcare and a rigged economy, to scrutinizing our higher education system or institutions more broadly, each volume details some ten specific policy solutions promising to systemically treat the issue(s), transforming the problem at a lasting *structural* level, not just a superficial one. These innovative and disruptive policy solutions flow from the authors' research, knowledge and experience, but they are especially characterized by their unflinching commitment to our collective normative understanding of who we can and ought to be.

What the individual volumes aim to offer, then, are navigable road maps for how we may begin to overcome the many specific challenges that we face, guiding us towards new ways of working cooperatively to rise above our differences, heal the wounds in our communities, recalibrate our modes of governance, and revitalize our institutions. Cumulatively, however, they achieve something of even greater synergy, greater import: they reconstruct that India of our imagination, of our aspirations, the India reflected in the constitutional preamble that we all surely want to be a part of.

Let us put aside that depiction of a mirror with an enemy staring back at us. Instead, together, we help to construct a whole new set of images. One where you may look at your nation and see your individual identity and dignity reflected in it, and when you look within your individual self, you may find the pride of your nation residing there.

Aakash Singh Rathore, Mridula Mukherjee, Pushparaj Deshpande and Syeda Hameed

Introduction

In the run-up to the 2017 Gujarat Assembly elections, the then Congress President Rahul Gandhi's visit to the iconic Somnath Temple was embedded with profound meanings. The scion of the Gandhi family had no qualms about performing aarti, as his party rebutted the suspicions surrounding his beliefs. Beyond the usual business of sneers and jibes that election campaigns invariably involve, the stopover at the temple was a reminder of the distance that secularism as an idea and practice has travelled. The visit to this temple was significant as discussions on secularism as statecraft in India have long been inflected by the debate surrounding the reconstruction of Somnath, which involved the participation of some of the key members of India's first prime minister Jawaharlal Nehru's cabinet—home minister Vallabhbhai Patel and food and agriculture minister K.M. Munshi. In his memoir, Munshi recalls Nehru's displeasure at what he termed revivalist activity while a defiant Munshi preferred to see it as 'collective subconscious' of the nation.[1] Nevertheless, on the advice of Mahatma Gandhi, a devout Hindu and an indisputable nationalist, the temple reconstruction was made to be a private endeavour, not funded by the state. Later, there was another twist to the tale when Rajendra Prasad, the then head of the state, agreed to inaugurate the renovated temple despite a cautionary note from Nehru. Prasad's response opens up the debate on the typically Indian brand of secularism: 'I would do the same with a mosque or a church if I were invited.' He added: 'This is the core of Indian secularism. Our state is neither irreligious nor anti-religious.'[2]

Another temple has been at the heart of the secularism debate for decades. With the pronouncement by a Constitution Bench of the Supreme Court in the Ram Temple–Babri Masjid title suit, the entire portion of land at the centre of the dispute has been handed over to Ram Lalla Virajman through his 'next friend'. Nearly twenty-eight years after the Karsevaks pulled down the Babri Masjid, the apex court has obliterated it as a legal entity attached to the land on which it stood. It has, however, directed that a plot of five acres be provided to the Muslims to build a mosque. For liberal consciousness, disturbed by the hostile posturing of parties in dispute, this amounts to a 'closure', and what matters ultimately is 'peace', and the judgment, by its so-called 'balancing act', it is argued, promises that. Sadly, this whole argument rests on the goodwill and helplessness of the minorities caught in an increasingly majoritarian polity. While the judgment claims to have kept individual faith aside in pronouncing on a land dispute, it ultimately cedes to 'undisputed faith' rather than land and revenue records to determine adverse possession. In a nutshell, the end result of justice delivered is that triumphalism has prevailed. From the Somnath Temple to the Ram Temple, what distance has Indian secularism travelled between these years?

Minorities and the Secular Predicament

As we broach the subject of minorities, its inextricable bond with two allied ideas, equally foundational to the vision of the republic, ought not to be missed: secularism and nationalism. The three together form a conceptual whole to the extent that none finds its manifestation without reference to the other two. The minority question in India has several departures. For an archetypal nationalist, the very endurance of the subject post-Independence is a thorn in the flesh. The disapproval takes a variety of expressions: appeasement, vote banks, disaffection, or to quote a phrase, 'fissiparous tendencies'—a term invoked quite often in official parlance and public forums to denote secessionism and disunity among minority groups. The resilience of religions, customs and practices of non-Sanskritist or non-Hinduistic inheritance, considered perilous to national security, called for a final solution. In the early years, 'Indianization' was the resolution offered. The term largely worked as a floating signifier, where the signified could not be fixed. Since culture was the operative terrain, Indianization had a range of implications but largely emerged from the vision of the nation that was being proposed. Secular nationalist stream of thought relied on a modernist framework where tradition and affiliations termed primordial were devil incarnates, displayed little potential for reform, and were best done away with. Thus, personal laws were to be abrogated, religious schools frowned upon, and religiosity in the public arena discouraged. It was an idea whose origins could be traced to the French concept of *laïcité,* where a wall of separation was erected between the church and the state, the religious and the political. Proponents of this version of difference-blind secularism were drawn largely from the urbanized, English-speaking elite who despised everyday rituals and performative religiosity of the vernacular.

It was in the supremacist framework that Indianization found the most resounding reverberation, albeit with its own improvisations. It sought two kinds of convergences, nation with Hindu, and Hindu with Vedic/Sanskritic tradition. Accordingly, Vedic Aryans provided the 'substratum' on which India's national identity rested, the rest simply assimilated into it. It followed that the truly Indian way of life was the Hindu dharma that emanated from *Manusmriti,* and, which, according to Balraj Madhok, the leader of the Jan Sangh, who reflected at length on the subject, was secular in its essence. Indianization implied the adoption of the dharma by all other religious forms which were to exist as *panths* (sects). As a result, religions having their genesis in the Indian subcontinent, such as Jainism, Buddhism and Sikhism, termed Indic, are denied autonomy of existence and world view, and are usually characterized as offshoots of Hinduism.[3] The Indic or Hinduistic religions supposedly share religious philosophy, organizational structure and also religiously ordained political behaviour. In a nutshell, Indianization, as visualized by Madhok, was an assimilative process that disparaged the plurality of cultures, languages and religions adhering to exclusive identities, but most repugnant was the presence of Muslims, considered the source of all evils by the supremacist thought.[4]

At odds with these two divergent views has been the idea of secularism, nay pluralism, which revealed itself more in the form of practice as against mere theorization. The pluralist case claimed its proximity to vernacular religious forms, which were irreverent to the scriptural injunctions, and formed a shared discursive sphere. Historian Tara Chand records this confluence in his masterly work *Influence of Islam on Indian Culture*:

> [It] led to the development of a new culture which was neither exclusively Hindu nor purely Muslim. It was indeed a Muslim–Hindu culture. Not only did Hindu religion, Hindu art, Hindu literature and Hindu science absorb Muslim elements, but the very spirit of Hindu culture and the very stuff of Hindu mind were also altered, and the Muslim reciprocated by responding to the change in every department of life.[5]

It insisted on mutuality, tolerance and compositeness, and thus presented itself opposed to the secular modernists as much as against the cultural supremacists. With everyday religiosity as its point of departure, it revelled in, as indeed exaggerated, the idea of religious tolerance. Religion as faith, minus its ideological contamination, according to Ashis Nandy,[6] was what we needed to return to, in contrast to the abolitionist perspective of the secular modernists.

What was missed in this formulation was the potential of politics to reorient cultures—deploy selective symbols, harp on real or imagined fault lines, and forge artificial boundaries in accordance with its own requirements. Beyond the portrait of a largely idyllic and shared world of reciprocal exchanges, politics of culture works to reproduce hierarchies, build hegemonies, and rupture the everyday world of cultural coexistence. In the 1940 Lahore declaration of the Muslim League, Muhammad Ali Jinnah's presidential address—'Hindus and Muslims belong to two different religious philosophies, social customs, and literature . . . two different civilizations'[7]—stands as a repudiation of the centuries-long cultural process that theorists of pluralism have relied upon. Jinnah's two-nation theory received an unpredictable support from the Barelvi school, more closely associated with the everyday world of devotional (Sufi) Islam. In an identical process, the Hindutva expansionism today relies heavily on the co-option of Kabirpanthis in Uttar Pradesh and elsewhere, Namasudras in Bengal, followers of Chuharmal in Bihar or Basavanna in Karnataka, all considered rebels against Vedic Hinduism.

Underlying these contending visions of nationalism is the question of minority cultures. Should they be protected, allowed to flourish or be obliterated and assimilated in the national whole? There is convergence between the secular modernists and the diehard Hindutva nationalists in the sense that both prescribe assimilation—one into a modernist project, the other into a national culture primarily defined by Sanskritic Hinduism. Recent history is replete with such moments of congruence—the uniform civil code debate, state funding of minority institutions, modernization of seminaries, reservations for vulnerable minorities, and a host of other issues. The pluralist vision, on the other hand, tolerant of divergent practices, assumes cultures (and thereby religious observances) as frozen in time and space, and remains notoriously inattentive to currents of cultural change and transformation.

Who Is a Minority?

In a country marked by multiplicity of faiths, speeches, castes, ethnicities and geographies, the question 'who is a minority?' is riddled with complexities. What adds to the intricacy is that each of these collectivities is segmented into status groups, sects, forms of worship, and regional variations to the extent that the difference offsets the commonality. Identities are multiple, and each of these intersects with the other to complicate the situation further. A Santhal convert to Christianity bears no resemblance to the Syrian Christians in Kerala, be it in language, custom or the status that she enjoys in the wider society. A Tamil Muslim has far more points of interaction with a Tamil Hindu than with his co-religionists in Kashmir and in Urdu-speaking areas. This is a complexity that afflicts the formation of majority identity as much. Minorities are contextually produced, and violence is key to it: Biharis in Maharashtra, Tamil speakers in Karnataka during the language riots, Bengalis in Assam at the peak of the Assam movement, Sikhs in 1984. On similar grounds, the rise of Hindutva nationalism in India corresponds with the exclusion and demonization of and the use of targeted violence against the Muslims, and occasionally the Christians.

The South African experience reminds us that statistics alone do not take us too far in defining a minority. The relationship between the minority and the majority is mediated by power and politics. Historically, these are not perpetually stable categories, and an alteration, even inversion, of the dominant–subordinate relationship is not so uncommon. The White settlers in Zimbabwe comprising a mix of British-Irish, Afrikaans and Greek-Portuguese, aided by liberal land grants and other privileges showered to them by the colonial regime, dominated Zimbabwean society and economy. Their minoritization began with the end of the apartheid regime and the rise of nativist politics. By the same token, Kashmiri Pandits, once dominant, discovered themselves as a minority with the rise of separatism in the state.

India represents one of the most complex multinational and polyethnic societies to be governed by modern democratic structures. The presence of at least 1600 speech communities has been recorded by the Indian census, of which at least thirty-three are more than one million strong. More than 3000 castes and nearly 350 tribal groupings form the Indian cultural mosaic. Further, the adherents of almost all the world's major religions—Judaism, Christianity, Islam, Hinduism, Jainism, Buddhism, Sikhism, Zoroastrianism and various forms of animism—are to be found here. About 80 per cent of the population practises Hinduism, which in itself is a highly plural system of beliefs and practices. The disaggregation of the population along regions and religions provides an intriguing scenario. There are merely 2.3 per cent Christians in the country, but they form the majority in three states, namely Meghalaya, Mizoram and Nagaland, and are a significant proportion of the population in Kerala, Arunachal Pradesh and Manipur. One of the most prosperous states of India, Punjab, has a Sikh majority. The Indian Muslim population, though only 14.1 per cent according to the latest census, constitutes the third highest in the world in its sheer magnitude. Given the situation, quite often, the neat compartmentalization of majority and minority appears mythical. Stretching the argument to an absurd extent, a single-judge bench of an Indian court declared in 2007 that Hindus were a true minority if caste and sectarian divisions were to be taken into account. The judge's order read that Muslims were in fact the 'only majority religious community in comparison with other religious communities', and all others were 'in minority comparison to the Muslims of India'.[8] Mercifully, realizing the preposterousness of the order, and its far-reaching consequences, a division bench of the high court swiftly overturned it.

From a strictly juristic reading, the Constitution of India recognizes religious and linguistic minorities for the purpose of conferring special rights to establish educational institutions of their choice. Articles 29 and 30 carry the empowering provisions in this regard. The reticence of the Constitution-makers in defining who constitutes a minority has led to endless litigation. Were they to be decided numerically? Given India's federalism, were the minorities to be determined at the level of the state or at the national plane? Clarity on this account was pertinent because, as mentioned above, there are states, though small in size, but with a predominant population of 'religious minorities'. The question 'who would constitute a disempowered minority in Punjab, Jammu and Kashmir, Mizoram, Meghalaya and Nagaland?' required an exercise of the mind. This question acquired far more significance in case of linguistic minorities residing in states carved out on the basis of language. Two apex court judgments, read simultaneously, sought to resolve the problem—*Kerala Education Bill v. Unknown*[9] held minorities to be those comprising less than 50 per cent of the population, and the *T.M.A. Pai* judgment[10] settles the determination of minorities at the level of the state. However, problems remain. The attempts to resolve definitional ambiguity have led to an anarchic situation in which virtually every community could claim minority status, thus leaving the majority a redundant entity.

Obfuscation of the minority question comes from yet another quarter as sundry vulnerabilities come to be amassed under a single conceptual canopy—the minority. Sometime back, women, irrespective of their ethnic or racial origins, were termed as a minority. More recently the term 'sexual minority' has come into popular usage to refer to the disparate community of non-heterosexual orientations. Often, disability too is brought under the rubric of minority. This elasticity in usage runs the risk of the concept losing its specificity, its history, and thereby, the message that it carries. For the purpose of this volume, we have consciously confined the term to its historical origins to refer to threatened cultural collectives. Beyond constitutional provisions, and conceptually speaking, there are broadly three kinds of minorities in most plural societies. 'Nationalities' demand self-governance rights over the part of national territory that they consider as their homeland. A handful of them, not all, see secessionism as the only course. The creation of ethnic homelands such as Bodoland, Nagaland and Mizoram was India's response to ethnic upsurges in the north-east as a militaristic approach could deliver little result. The indigenous groups or tribes seek protection of their language, script, ideas of religion as well as their land and territory. Schedule 5 and Schedule 6 areas privilege the right of ethnic groups over land and resources, apart from reservations for Scheduled Tribes in public employment, political offices and educational institutions. Minorities of the third kind are dispersed ones who do not have exclusive claims over land or territory. Religious communities as well as language speakers residing outside their 'homeland' could be termed as dispersed ones. Their expectations range from cultural protection, preservation of identity and security to a share in national wealth and resources.

There are numerous kinds of minorities, but admittedly, the religious minorities preoccupy most discussions on the subject. If Partition violence scarred our collective quest for nationhood, the targeted pogroms that were orchestrated from time to time—Bhiwandi (1970), Mumbai (1992–93), Bhagalpur (1989), Nellie (1983), Delhi (1984), Gujarat (2002), among many others—serve to fortify boundaries and reinforce a divided existence. More insidious is the structural violence, which is normalized and rendered quotidian, that sections of religious minorities bear. Muslims, most populous among them, are sparsely represented in formal, salaried employment, while they are disproportionately present in the informal sector as well as among those self-employed as automobile mechanics, vendors, fruit and vegetable sellers, masons, carpenters, welders, repair shop owners. A recent National

Sample Survey Office survey revealed that out of every 1000 urban Muslim males in the employable age, only 288 (249 females) could find a regular job. Corresponding figures from other communities were as follows: Christians (494 for males and 647 among females), Hindus (463 males and 439 females) and Sikhs (418 males and 482 females). Caught in a vicious circle of low educational attainment and poverty levels, their material vulnerability found no signs of improvement even when the Indian economy registered the fastest growth.[11]

Marginalization takes various forms, and for Muslims in particular it is cumulative in nature. India, as elsewhere, is witnessing a rising tide of majoritarianism, the brunt of which is borne by ordinary Muslims. Politics is double-edged; while it fortifies boundaries when adopting a communitarian course, it also allows for the building of bridges as an antidote to supremacist inclinations. The 2014 and 2019 elections in India were a watershed. A right-wing government established itself at the Centre and in most states, and as a corollary, the minority political voice was left redundant. The Bharatiya Janata Party (BJP) won in constituencies where minorities mattered; it also won in places where they had little presence. True to its ideological make-up, it fielded no Muslim candidate in the 2014 elections, and only one in 2019. All this while, our media discourse, aided by fly-by-night psephologists, busied itself in inventing minority/Muslim vote banks where none existed.

The Question of Loyalty

The nation state and the minority cultures residing within it are almost eternally in a fraught relationship. At the heart of it is the question of allegiance, the terminal loyalty that the state wishes to command. Minorities insisting on the distinctiveness of their identity and practices are unfailingly the usual suspects. The problem compounds when cultural minorities are considered to have 'kin states' in the neighbourhood. Urdu-speaking Muslims are accused of nursing divided loyalties, and therefore the Hindutva catchphrase 'go to Pakistan.' Bengali-speaking Muslims in Assam carry the burden of being Bangladeshis. Conceivably, it was this intricacy of the situation that prompted the early leaders of India and Pakistan to enter into an agreement promising mutual comfort to their respective minority populations. The Nehru–Liaquat Pact (1950) between the prime ministers of the two countries assured protection of life, liberty and equal rights to the religious minorities and paved the way for the setting up of minority commissions in the two states.

The question of loyalty poses varied political responses ranging from complaints of deep-seated prejudice, intolerance and discrimination to execution of extreme violence bordering on genocide. The examples are simply far too many. In India, for instance, a sort of 'religious profiling' in counterterror operations has been written about. Renewed demands for Muslims to make a visible demonstration of their allegiance to India are disturbingly frequent. Hindus in Bangladesh; Christians, Ahmadiyyas and Shias in Pakistan; and Rohingyas in Myanmar continue to suffer targeted violence. In Sri Lanka, the militaristic solution to the existing nationality upsurge led to the killing of tens of thousands of Tamils. In neighbouring Bangladesh, the predicament of a Bengali or Bangladeshi nationalism has failed to address the citizenship quest of its religious and ethnic minorities. Most striking is the case of its Urdu-speaking population, which, having survived extreme violence, has been left stateless, bereft of constitutional entitlements. The Nepalese-speaking population in apparently peaceful Bhutan has been forced to leave the country, only to end up as refugees in Nepal.

In the majoritarian framework, loyalty is hierarchized. Not all minorities are under perpetual surveillance. In the cultural construction of Hindutva, the Indic communities rate higher in the fidelity graph as against the non-Indics. Madhok's Indianization project equated Hinduism with nationalization, and picked on the Muslims, the Communists and the Christians, in that order, for their extraterritorial loyalty. No such programme was designed for the Sikhs, the Buddhists, the Jains, who for Madhok were sects of the Hindu dharma. The Indic/non-Indic duality comes to inform the framing of policies and promulgation of laws. Clause 3 of the Presidential Order of 1950 restricts the Scheduled Caste (SC) category to only caste groups from the Hindu religion. Two amendments, one in 1956 and the other in 1990, paved the way for the inclusion of Mazhabi Sikhs and neo-Buddhists, while Muslim and Christian low castes have been left to battle it out in the courts. A close reading of the case law on the subject shows how courts have restored SC status to converts returning into the Hindu fold, but continue to deny the same to low-caste converts to non-Indic religions. The 2006 Gujarat Freedom of Religion Bill made a similar distinction among religions. Clubbed into one group, Hindus, Sikhs, Jains and Buddhists could convert from one to the other without restriction, as could the various sects among Christians and Muslims. But any attempt to convert from an Indic to a non-Indic religion (or vice versa) had impediments at every step, including the threat of incarceration. The Rajasthan government proposed an identical bill, with the apparent aim of checking conversion by 'inducement, allurement and force'. Both the bills, however, failed to secure presidential assent, and were eventually withdrawn. The Citizenship Amendment Act, 2019, accords citizenship to non-Muslim immigrants from Pakistan, Bangladesh and Afghanistan on the grounds of them being subjected to religious persecution in their home countries.

A Volume on Minorities: Text and Context

At the outset, a couple of disclaimers are in order. The foremost one is that the essays included in the volume have no academic pretensions, rather they lie at the cross section of social criticism, intellectual reflections and hands-on suggestions on the subject.

Neither does the volume authoritatively claim to exhaust the subject of minorities in its entirety. Further, the contributors are drawn from varied professional settings and training—lawyers, journalists, development researchers, civil society activists and academics—all seized of the pressing questions of our times, the foremost being the rising tide of majoritarianism. The underlying consensus, though unstated, is that the recent ferocious turn in Indian polity, insofar as the minorities are concerned, is neither abrupt nor transient. Its roots lie in the state practices of the past, in the scheme outlays, in the counterterror operations, in the framing of our educational policies, in the exclusionary practices in the labour market, in the impunities extended to perpetrators of mass violence, in the ethnicization of body politics. Most of the essays then search for a plausible solution that an analysis of what went wrong can offer. The past is therefore a storehouse for the future, for hope.

There has been of late a veritable industry centring on the fate of liberal democracies—none more influential and evocative than David Runciman's book *How Democracy Ends*.[12] The coming to power of authoritarian, right-wing parties and leaders across the swathes of what were the cradles of liberal democracies has invoked the spectre of 1930s Europe which witnessed the rising tide of Nazism and Fascism, and which swept Hitler and Mussolini to power. There is little agreement on whether what we are seeing is simply a repeat of the politics of inter-war years (Runciman says no), or whether the threats to democracy are quite unique—aided in no small measure by the rise and unprecedented spread of technology.

Amir Ali's piece can be located in this stream of literature reflecting on the present and future of democracy. His contribution to the debate is on specifically how these democracies are morphing into brute majoritarian ones, where the voice of the ethnic and religious minorities is not only silenced and rendered redundant, but its very silencing becomes central to the crafting of the majority. The state becomes unabashedly majoritarian and the rhetoric of divisiveness and even hate comes to be established and normalized at the heart of institutions once avowedly secular and plural.

Ali fears that once the minorities have been disenfranchised through insidious means—whether or not their right to vote exists becomes moot because the efficacy of their vote has been wholly negated— the state would move in to strip them of the rights guaranteed under the Constitution. Ali shows how the rhetoric of right-wing leaders and those holding high office has targeted minority rights as 'appeasement'.

What gives, then? Are we to reconcile ourselves with this gloomy scenario and await the unfolding of the worst? Despite himself, Ali sees the possibility of revitalizing the core kernel of democracy and the values that surround it. And if the state is turning away from the values of democracy, it is up to us, he says, to actively counter the hatred all around with attempts at empathy. It may not yet be too late to invoke a spirit of mutual reconciliation.

One such attempt at mutual reconciliation is the Karwan-e-Mohabbat (Caravan of Love) campaign—ordinary people travelling to the homes of those who have been killed or lynched in hate violence carried out in the name of cow protection, in a kind of pilgrimage of atonement. Navsharan Singh, one of the travellers on this journey, recounts her meetings with the widows and mothers of those killed and maimed, of a community beaten into submission— as much by the violence as by the apathy, indeed active resentment of the state's agencies. It is a depressing catalogue that she unfurls for us. She shows us how the machinery of hate and kill is coordinated; how the gau rakshak, a lumpen private vigilante, is absorbed as an agent of the state through the issuance of government identity cards and through a plethora of institutions such as the cow commissions set up by state governments. Singh is quick to point out that cow vigilantism and its concomitant violence is not simply socio-cultural but has a distinct economic dimension. Muslims (and Dalits) form the bulk of those engaged in cattle trade, and the new policies and institutions actively serve to break the commercial backs of these communities. Thus, they now face impoverishment coupled with the omnipresent threat of mob violence.

If there is the spectacular violence of the lynch mob, there is too the dull, routine, everyday discrimination—of being denied housing, education, employment, based on reasons never stated openly, but subtly communicated. Farah Naqvi looks at one of the novel recommendations made by the Sachar Committee (2006) which marked a vital discursive shift—the Equal Opportunity Commission (EOC). This was to be a body that would address a range of discriminations across sections—not just for Muslims or minorities. Naqvi says that this, backed by an overarching legal, definitional and procedural framework, could have offered a holistic institutional response to a multitude of discriminations faced by a range of socially marginalized groups. It could have bridged the fractured and ad hoc nature of remedies available through different commissions and offices. The moment was however lost when the Menon Committee in 2008 proposed an infirm EOC bill, and turf wars between commissions ensued alongside. The question to ask too is if that moment has been lost forever. A government which governs in the name of 'sabka saath, sabka vikaas'—purportedly a slogan guaranteeing development and prosperity to all, but is in fact meant to be a corrective to so-called appeasements and imagined injustices of the past secular regimes—will perforce be wilfully blind to the discrimination that the marginalized face.

The entanglements between religion and economy are rarely examined. Here, Barbara Harriss-White undertakes a masterly survey of the 'ways in which religions structure Indian capitalism'. Her focus is on the informal economy, which remains outside the purview of the state's regulatory practices, allowing religion greater sway over the process of accumulation. She traces the overlaps between the complex forms of social–cultural differentiation among different minority groups, their religious beliefs and their economic differentiation. She calls attention, for example, to the absence of social obligations and notions of ritual purity and pollution that allow localized Muslim groups to engage in innovative economic activity, or the extent to which religious observances and closed marriage and kin ties lead to capital accumulation among the Jains. Bringing in questions of caste, *biradari*, community and secularism, Harriss-White weaves a rich tapestry explaining the interweaving of religious plurality and commerce, thus offering a timely and necessary corrective to mainstream economic literature.

The relationship between law and minorities is a vexed one. On the one hand, constitutional guarantees in the form of Articles 29 and 30, dealing specifically with minority rights, in addition to Article 14 (right to equality) etc., provide a sound legal scaffolding to protect minorities. This was a pact the postcolonial state made with its minorities—and which also distinguished it from many other newly born nation states emerging from the dust and debris of colonization. On the other hand, however, the law can also work to disenfranchise and disempower. Three essays look at the transactions between cultural constructions and legislation. The triple talaq bill passed by both houses into law, the Muslim Women (Protection of Rights on Marriage) Act, 2019, was the culmination of a legal process triggered by a reference to the chief justice of India by a two-judge bench of the Supreme Court to examine discriminatory practices within Muslim personal law in 2015. It has a much longer history of trading in tropes—the most popular being the sexually lascivious Muslim male, the disempowered Muslim woman bereft of agency, and an unreformed and frozen Muslim personal law. When popular stereotypes dominate legislative business, the question of reform fades into oblivion to be replaced by a punitive regime.

A key interlocutor in the triple talaq debate is Flavia Agnes, who brings her experience of working with women survivors of domestic violence—of all faiths—and has been an advocate of incremental reform within all personal law systems over the hegemonic idea of a 'uniform' civil code. In her essay, she contextualizes the passage of the bill in the history of reform of Muslim personal laws, demolishing many commonly held prejudices, while demonstrating the veritable minefield that Muslim women who seek justice have to negotiate.

One of the most potent illustrations of stereotypes congealing in and through the law is the anti-terror legislation, which while putatively neutral, serves to criminalize certain socio-religious groups. Manisha Sethi shows us the workings of these laws—from the Terrorist and Disruptive Activities (Prevention) Act (TADA) to the Prevention of Terrorism Act (POTA) and the Unlawful Activities Prevention Act (UAPA)—and how they tend to reify communities and assign properties to social groups. The structure of these laws, which recognize and foreground guilt by association, and the widespread prosecution—though not necessarily conviction—of those belonging to certain caste and community groups end up creating suspect communities very much in the manner that the colonial Criminal Tribes Act, 1871, created 'hereditary criminals'. The figure of the Islamist terrorist, as an 'essential type', ought to be seen as much a product of the law as of popular culture and politics.

Tanweer Fazal traces the career of the notion and substance of citizenship as it was delineated and defined by our Constitution-drafters. Despite majoritarian calls for privileging Hindu or, more broadly, Indic religions on the lines of Israel, *jus soli* (right of soil) rather than *jus sanguine* (right of blood) became the basis of citizenship. From time to time, this universal definition of citizenship has received challenges from nativist movements, but it appears to be under the greatest strain at the present moment. Two developments threaten to hollow it out. The first is the recently concluded National Register of Citizens (NRC) to detect undocumented migrants in Assam, which has left a staggering 19 lakh people staring at the possibility of statelessness. Fazal argues that the migrant/foreigner is not an empty signifier but is filled with ethnic markers, identified most naturally and forcefully with the Miya, the Muslim 'Bangladeshi'. Indeed, this is reinforced even further in the attempts to amend the Citizenship Act, which would *lawfully* differentiate between migrants/asylum-seekers on the basis of religion, welcoming the adherents of Indic religions alone. At the heart of this proposed amendment is the belief that India is the *natural* abode and home of Hindus to which they could return any time. Hindus alone are its authentic nationals. It indeed extends the provision to Sikhs, Buddhists, Jains and also Christians, but certainly not to Muslims.

The case of Kashmiri Pandits complicates the picture of the linkages between a minority and a hegemonic nation state. Numerically, the Pandits are indeed a minority. However, as Ankur Datta reminds us in his piece, their minority-ness is moulded 'by their spatial and political location in a region marked by dispute, violence, conflict and displacement since the end of colonialism in South Asia'. Their sense of self is marked by victimhood but also by a mobilization of a history and possibility of success. Especially interesting is the Pandits' relationship to Indian politics—a sense of pride about Nehru, identification (by themselves or by others) with Hindu nationalism, and their local conflict with Dogra interests in Jammu. The case of the Pandits alerts us to the complex ways in which minorities are conceived and the nuance that must accompany our understanding and conceptualization of minority.

The fate of the Urdu language is often tied erroneously to that of the community, namely Muslims. Data points to its decline and possible slow death; indeed, its impending death has been announced repeatedly, and its epitaph written over and over again. To be sure, there also seems to be a revival of Urdu language and *adab* (which could be loosely translated as literature but has a thicker meaning indicating deportment, etiquette, etc.)—as reflected in the popularity of, say, Rekhta (an annual Urdu literary programme in Delhi). Mahtab Alam brings a fresh perspective to understanding the crisis that grips the language. Reducing it to poetry sessions—mushairas and mehfils—will be to ensure its decimation. Alam argues instead to turn it into a language of utility. Urdu should be taught not as literature alone but should be the medium of instruction in schools and educational institutions. In other words, Urdu should be treated as a mother tongue rather than just a language of a religious, cultural or linguistic minority group. To this end, he offers us some practical solutions, which educationists, publishers and promoters of the language—sarkari as well as non-sarkari—would do well to note.

But perhaps, to speak of Urdu as a mother tongue in which modern education could be imparted is much more difficult than reducing it to an artefact. Azra Razzack and Muzna F. Alvi in their essay show how education, starting from the early years after Independence, was one of the primary sites of forging an Indian identity, which, however, shunned the diversity of language, region or caste. Alam has already noted how Urdu speakers were wary of returning to the language as their mother tongue. While the educational discourse was suspicious of what it termed 'narrow' and 'petty' loyalties, Muslim educational backwardness has only been met by the state through its schemes of madrasa modernization. Razzack and Alvi lament that Article 30, meant to bestow on minorities the right to establish and administer their own educational institutions, has been used as an alibi by governments to wash their hands of the task of Muslim education—leaving these children to make do with 'modern madrasas', skill development and vocational courses, which would allow them at best to secure petty employment in the job market, but effectively block social and educational mobility.

In its cognitive framework, the volume privileges the material lives of the minority groups over the spiritual or the cultural. In the real world, the two spheres rarely exist in compartments. Nonetheless, the task is to identify vulnerabilities that encumber the quest for the realization of substantive citizenship by minority groups. The essays therefore singularly emphasize educational attainment, employment prospects in a liberalized economy, possibilities of equal opportunity, violence of the state and vigilante groups, emerging questions of citizenship and employment, linking language with the material lives of its speakers, and document the receding political voice of minorities in times of a majoritarian upswing.

Disenfranchised Minorities, Dysfunctional Democracies

Amir Ali

Those of us who thought that there was an exceptionalism to Indian democracy may need to think again. The 2019 Parliamentary election results in India seem to conform to the predominant global trend of right-wing authoritarian populist governments being voted into power. In this upsurge of right-wing authoritarianism, what democracies are clearly not representing are the voices of religious, ethnic and other minorities. Furthermore, they are actively suppressing voices of liberal dissent. This essay expresses a certain caution towards democratic verdicts across the world that have returned right-wing authoritarian populist regimes. Such democratic upsurges are wreaking havoc on the fragile equipoise of democratic institutions, such as assertive election commissions, independent judiciaries and free presses. They have been helped along by the rise of social media that has in turn undermined the staid, respectable quality of traditional media that may have had some semblance of independence and freedom.

One would normally consider a democratic upsurge to be something of positive value. However, the manner in which the term 'democratic upsurge' is used here suggests a danger that seems to inhere within democracy. This is the tendency of the elective component of democracy to grow at the cost of other components such as the constitutional, which frequently checks the irrational excesses of the elective. In short, democratic upsurges across the world are destroying the very constitutional breakwaters that had been put in place to prevent them from wreaking too much havoc. One can perhaps, just for a moment, be allowed to agree with the wisdom of a philosopher such as Plato, when he expressed his disdain towards democracy. The *momentary* agreement with Plato is emphasized here, as Plato's disdain for democracy was completely dismissive.[1]

The disdain that some of us may have developed for democracy in the last few years cannot afford to be completely dismissive of the idea. It must be oriented towards revitalizing and reinstituting democracy, not by 'going back', as the word reinstitute may suggest. Rather it will have to reinstate democracy by retaining the core kernel of democracy and then surrounding and adding to that core kernel, some vital elements that either went missing or were never put there in the first place. This continued even as we went along singing paeans of glory to democracy all these years. The purpose of this essay is to reflect on what these elements are that have to be put in place in the crucial 'surround' around the core kernel of democracy.

The effect of this has been that we have been led up the garden path of democracy, without noticing that it has become an instrument in the systematic persecution of minorities. Here, I attempt to speculate about the course that democracies across the world will likely take, especially with regard to ethnic and religious minorities. I will take a rather pessimistic worst-case scenario, suggesting that increasingly, major democracies across the world, including India, are likely to experience extremely active persecution against minorities that may manifest itself in gruesome violence and pogroms against them.

The Priestcraft of Political Theory

One quick note may be added to the point on singing hymns of praise to democracy made in the preceding paragraph. At the risk of appearing overly critical of my own profession of political science, and more specifically political theory, I would hazard to suggest that the latter has increasingly resembled the practice and profession of priestcraft. There exists a pantheon of political concepts, foremost among them being democracy and civil society, which have been traded in and regularly paid obeisance to. This became especially pronounced in the three decades since the fall of the Berlin Wall and the collapse of many East European socialist command economies in 1989.

One of the sacred unions that was effected by the priestcraft was the marriage of democracy with the market, which was another one of the very powerful conceptual gods in the pantheon. Their marriage gave us market-democracy—a union in which democracy 'faithfully' replicated within itself the processes of the market. Having done so, democracy proceeded to sell itself to the highest bidder. Thus, democracies across the world were hijacked by a combination of coarse political rhetoric and very large amounts of purchasing power.

Let me reiterate one of the central arguments of this essay. Democracies are singularly failing to represent the voices and viewpoints of especially ethnic and religious minorities. Furthermore, they are working to actively disenfranchise them and render them redundant. In the case of India, the manner in which the BJP has 'polarized' the electorate, it is actively ensuring that the Muslim vote just does not matter. The message of the redundant Muslim vote that is sent out is unequivocal and clear. In the chilling message that this conveys, there is also a kind of 'your time is up' warning, when the no-nonsense manner of the present is contrasted with that of supposed 'appeasement' of past Congress regimes.

This essay pessimistically, yet with the hope that its viewpoint is proven wrong, suggests that there is a frightening momentum that democracy in India and across the world has acquired. In doing so, democracy has been placed on an unstoppably dangerous and adventurist path. There seems little possibility of effecting a course correction. As the rolling stones of democracies across the world gather momentum, they can only end in a large crash that brings about the end and demise of democracy itself.

The political theorist Mark Chou has suggested that democracies contain within themselves the seeds of their own destruction and are thereby prone to killing themselves.[2] The imagery of democratic rolling stones, hurtling down treacherously steep polities, is meant to be a graphic portrayal of such suicidal tendencies. It can also be suggested that in the latter half of the twentieth century and the first two decades of the twenty-first century, the proliferation and profusion of democracies that we experienced was but a brief interlude. Democracies were propped up and retained by a curious combination of carbon energy technologies, their machinery and associated financial arrangements. US-led hegemony ensured that it had a vested interest in creating carbon copies of democracy across the world.[3] Since that hegemonic order is changing, we may witness the very demise of democracy as we know it. The accompanying dislocation in terms of violent upheaval is likely to be extremely disturbing.

The Fate of Disenfranchised Minorities

What will be the fate of disenfranchised minorities in dysfunctional democracies? To begin with, there will inevitably be the calling into question of minority rights provisions. Such provisions were designed and entrenched in most liberal constitutions in a way that they were kept safe, just beyond the irresponsible reach of the kind of authoritarian democratic upsurges that we are witnessing across the world. The stage for the actual dislodging of these constitutional provisions is prepared by some of the most atrocious and base political rhetoric that is clearly incendiary. In India and across the world, there are numerous examples of holders of high political office literally shooting their mouths off with words that are intended to shock and provoke.

There are broadly three kinds of responses to an instance of verbal abuse of this kind. There are the vehement expressions of opposition and demands for apology that are made by centrist and centre-left politicians. Those on the extreme right of the political spectrum will usually express a kind of indifferent nonchalance to these remarks, which is a kind of implicit support to the sentiments behind them. Then there are politicians on the centre right who will express some degree of reservation to the remarks being made, but would want to brush them aside, or make light of them, by suggesting that the words are inconsequential. The net effect of all three positions is to allow unhindered the expression of hate speech, consequently resulting in an unbridled spiral that makes democratic discourse thoroughly despicable. One immediate effect of this spiral is to ensure the electoral success of right-wing authoritarian populist parties. It can be suggested that the recourse to atrocious political rhetoric and hate speech is a rational calculation on the part of demagogues to enhance electoral prospects.

This is most clearly visible in the case of President Donald Trump in the USA when he recently suggested that four Democratic congresswomen, Alexandria Ocasio-Cortez, Ilhan Omar, Rashida Tlaib and Ayanna Pressley, go back to where they came from. Many have wondered at this particular proclivity of the US president to speak and tweet irresponsible things about people and events. There is perhaps method in this madness. Every single verbal outrage shores up President Trump's electoral prospects. In other words, there is a *base instinct* of the electorate that politicians such as Trump appeal to whenever they engage in the kind of verbal spats that they are associated with. The vast majority of Trump's targets happen to be ethnic minorities and

Muslims. Trump has been widely noted for the manner in which he has denounced London mayor Sadiq Khan.[4] In doing so, he is appealing to the Islamophobic elements in his core constituency.

What is worrying is the manner in which the supposedly saner and more responsible elements in the Republican Party have remained silent or chosen to conveniently look away. The House of Representatives condemned Trump's outburst against the four Democratic congresswomen on 16 July 2019. The vast majority of Republican members in the House of Representatives did not vote to condemn Trump's boorish behaviour.[5] There is a very clear burial of decency in the mad frenzy that democracies across the world are caught up in. This indecency manifests itself in outright abuse and hatred of the kind engaged in by Trump and supported by members of the Republican Party. It also reveals that the Republican Party continues to close ranks behind someone as controversial and divisive as Donald Trump. In doing so, it continues to fail to play what political scientists Steven Levitsky and Daniel Ziblatt call an effective 'gatekeeping' role. What this means is that much before Trump's becoming the US President, the vast majority of members of the Republican Party failed to act as gatekeepers to prevent the rise of such a controversial figure. This ineffective gatekeeping continues to plague the Republican Party, as the decision by the vast majority of Republicans in the House of Representatives to not condemn Trump reveals. This is done either out of pusillanimity or the myopic desire to win the next elections, or both. Either way it will, according to Levitsky and Ziblatt's argument, result in the death of democracy.[6]

In India, we have a slightly different situation. It is not Prime Minister Narendra Modi who directly engages in hate speech. The recourse to such incendiary remarks is frequently and routinely taken by other members of the BJP—the most recent example being the prime accused in the Malegaon terror attack, Sadhvi Pragya, who won the Bhopal parliamentary seat in the 2019 elections.[7] In the face of numerous outrageous remarks, the prime minister usually maintains an indifferent, almost stoic, sage-like silence that seems to suggest that he is pained by what he hears. After the liberal media has expressed some degree of outrage, Prime Minister Modi has been known to issue words of condemnation—a case of too little and too late. This is a pattern that can be discerned from the early half of Modi's first tenure, and can be seen especially since the killing of Mohammad Akhlaque in September 2015.

The strategy seems to be that the prime minister does not really want to reprimand his firebrand lieutenants. What the liberal appeal to the prime minister needing to speak out misses completely is Modi's own track record. Many of his remarks prior to the outbreak of the 2002 Gujarat riots were of an irresponsible nature, unbecoming of an occupant of the office of the chief minister. Subsequently, his insensitive remarks about those who had been displaced by the riots and were living in refugee camps can hardly be considered to have had a healing effect.[8]

The picture that we have then of disenfranchised minorities in democracies is one in which they serve as electoral cannon fodder for political parties that want to consolidate the vote of dominant majorities. Their disenfranchisement is premised upon the notion that they are a threat. The threat is itself a political spectre deliberately created to consolidate the majority and rally it around the idea that something has to be done to show these people their place. A large part of Modi's success, despite a patchy governance and economic record, even by his own standards, has been his ability to supposedly show Muslims their place at the margins.

As has been mentioned a number of times, the developments in democracy in India, whereby a party like the BJP is able to perfect the art of winning elections so emphatically, are also a confirmation of a worldwide trend. What is happening in India is something that is being experienced in varying degrees in most major democracies across the world. It is precisely the global nature of this trend that makes things more difficult and dangerous. The reason for this is that the worsening climate of democracy across the world will ensure that international public opinion will continue to look the other way when debased democracies proceed to heap atrocities on their most vulnerable sections. This is likely to continue to escalate from verbal abuse to actual physical attacks that may be sporadic and isolated in the beginning but are likely to acquire a more systematic and widespread character, if present trends continue. This continuous movement towards mass violence against minority groups is furthered by a conveniently complacent feeling that exists to the point of narcissism amongst democracies that they do not carry out major atrocities on vulnerable populations. It is only regimes of the extreme right-wing Augusto Pinochet variety in Chile that are extremely repressive or Stalinist regimes on the extreme left of the political spectrum that can match, if not exceed, such horrors. This is perhaps one of the most vain assumptions made by uncritical analysts of democracy.

I am arguing then that in order to understand what is happening to democracy, one has to first identify the core kernel of democracy, which would be the idea itself and the significance that the idea attaches to people's participation in their own government. It then has to be differentiated from the surround of democracy, which envelops and wraps itself around the core kernel. This democratic surround is analogous to a kind that keeps the kernel intact. Much in the way that the earth's atmosphere consists of the right mixture of various gases that then sustain life, it can be suggested what the democratic surround needs to consist of. Further, there are other elements that can be added to the democratic surround to make it more conducive to nurturing and sustaining the democratic core.

The current crises that democracies across the world are experiencing are a result of the depletion of the democratic surround—the most vital elements of which are rule of law, an independent judiciary, a free press, and an enlightened citizenry that is relatively free of stubborn prejudice. If one were to view this democratic surround as analogous to the atmospheric blanket that sustains life on the planet, it would almost be as if there is a continuous ratcheting up of the heat in the democratic surround. This heating of the democratic atmospheric surround is in large part contributed by vicious hate speech, which is reaching astonishingly toxic levels. It would of course be wrong to blame just majoritarian governments, who may be most responsible for these toxic emissions. There are also sections on the side of persecuted minorities who through their words and utterances may actually be further contributing to the heating up of the democratic surround. The case of the All India Majlis-e-Ittehad-ul-Muslimeen member of Parliament (MP) Asaduddin Owaisi may be interesting. While Owaisi speaks in a manner that is well versed with the legal intricacies of the Constitution, the effect of what he says is to further contribute to the overall polarization of our society. His younger brother Akbaruddin Owaisi engages in rhetoric that is far cruder.[9]

An Ethnic Democracy?

With this vitiation of the democratic surround, India seems to be increasingly moving towards what the Israeli sociologist Sammy Smooha calls an 'ethnic democracy' or a democracy whose attributes are completely defined by its majoritarian elements, often at the expense and exclusion of minority attributes.[10] Such a movement towards an ethnic democracy is helped along by a deteriorating situation within both India's Muslim minority and Hindu majority. Let us begin with the Muslim minority. While it is internally heterogeneous, the larger sense of victimhood within and victimization from without has meant that India's Muslims have become in the eyes of the vast majority of the people the biggest problem in the path of the nation advancing towards greatness.

Never in the more than seventy-year history of the Indian republic has the communal chasm between Hindus and Muslims been wider, to the point that it may now be almost unbridgeable.

It is not in the interest of any Indian, and for that matter anyone who believes in humanity's ability to get along with each other, for this gap to become wider. For the gap to be reduced it is imperative that there are people from both sides, Muslim and Hindu, who can sit down in a spirit of mutual reconciliation and not one of mutual recrimination. Remarkably, on both sides of the divide there are people who believe that their groups are the most victimized.

But the point here is that a genuine spirit of mutual reconciliation, which is never too late to invoke, may perhaps give rise, on both sides of the communal divide, to the realization of the baselessness of our many fears. Some people on the Muslim side may need to extend a hand in this mutual reconciliation, in the hope that there has to be a Hindu hand that will reach out and hold it. Indeed the firm belief, in the face of the hatred all around, that there will always be hands across communal divisions that can be held will be the first step in this process of healing and reconciliation.

What is being suggested then is that now is the time for people to actively counter hatred with attempts at empathy. Harsh Mander's Karwan-e-Mohabbat would be a good template, but is associated in the majoritarian imagination with always siding with Muslims.

A significant obstacle to this imperative to reconcile, however, is the mass mediatization of our society that drip-feeds individual imaginations with a constant supply of fears. There is the further omnipresence of social media, which will ensure that far from the kind of across-the-communal-divide reconciliation being suggested here, individuals are likely to wallow in their echo chambers, where the sum of their fears expands exponentially with the number of retweets and WhatsApp shares. In a plain-speaking age, when electorates seem to prefer leaders who can tell it like it is and call a spade a spade, it is vital for sensible individuals to do some plain speaking of their own and turn their backs on the antics of unprofessional television anchors. This is important as rates of news viewership have increased over the last few years, and what we may need is less rather than more news, especially of the irresponsible televised debate variety.

One of the things that obsessive news watching has done to people since the 9/11 attacks in New York is to convince them, by literally driving it into their heads, day in and day out, that terrorism is the biggest threat facing humanity. The statistical possibility of dying in a terror attack is certainly much lower than the kind of political energy that is invested in supposedly tackling it. One adds the 'supposedly' here because the good citizens of India and the world need to ask themselves if they can *really* trust political leaders who obsessively talk about countering terrorism and whose brash words are followed by impetuous, brash actions.

Far from stopping, the cycle of terrorism actually continues. The template of the global war on terrorism laid down by the US since 9/11 has harmed democracies through the infringement of civil liberties and the ramping up of securitization. It is astounding that many democracies across the world continue to endorse this manner of countering terrorism, whose efficacy is far from apparent and whose rhetoric far outstrips its actual ability to bring an end to the problem itself.

How Far Can Democracy Decline?

To get a sense of how grave a situation the current degeneration of democracy can bring about, democracies can be imagined as willing accomplices in crimes as serious as ethnic cleansing and large-scale massacres against vulnerable minorities. (This mode of thinking may be, in the opinion of some, rather alarmist.) The targeted minority group is likely to be portrayed as an enemy of the state, a supporter of terrorism, and perhaps in a slightly less extreme manner, as an irritant and impediment in the nation in question becoming great. The assertion of wanting to make a nation great may itself merely be a mask for a rampaging majoritarianism.

President Trump's assertions about making America great again are quite simply crude White supremacism. There is then an inherent racism in the numerous claims of wanting to make the country great.[11]

The leitmotif of making nations great usually arises from the right of the political spectrum. It can often be accompanied with a belief in free markets and free trade, and the restriction of outsiders and immigrants, who may sully the 'purity' of the nation. This assertion of greatness is quite extraordinary as it stems from political quarters that are the most constricted in terms of their outlook. There is a firm opposition to the generosity of welfare provisions. Welfare dependants are looked upon as despicable individuals whose existence is made possible by sponging off the largesse of welfare provisions. In India, for instance the word 'subsidy' has become a term of political abuse that is lobbed by the right-wing BJP, most often at students of Jawaharlal Nehru University (JNU). There is an almost Ayn Randian belief in the great virtue of individuals pulling themselves up by their own bootstraps and in the process contributing to the supposed greatness of the nation.

A lot of the Brexit debate on the 'leave' side in the UK partakes of the characteristics described here. There is an added belief that the bureaucratic obsession of the European Union is somehow inhibiting and stifling the inherent dynamism of 'Great Britain'. Margaret Thatcher is supposed to have put the 'Great' back into Britain.[12] In the case of the UK and the phenomenon of Thatcherism, it is interesting to note that assertions of greatness come into bolder relief against the backdrop of the petit-bourgeois class origins from where they are made.[13] It almost suggests a kind of correlation between the narrowness of the possibilities afforded by petit-bourgeois class origins, which almost seem to be seeking solace and compensation in the greatness of the nation. In the case of India and the aspirational middle class, which is a significant electoral prop for Modi, the aspirations themselves can hardly be said to have come to fruition, but there is an emphasis on the greatness of stature that India has achieved under Modi in the comity of nations.

In other words, repetitive assertions of greatness can be interpreted as dangerous signs of a potential fascism lurking within individuals. Wilhelm Reich, in his book *The Mass Psychology of Fascism*, suggests that fascism as a phenomenon cannot be considered unique to any nation. There is perhaps a fascism lurking in every single one of us. It takes the creation of the right political circumstances for this lurking individual fascism to assume a collective hold in the form of a mass psychology. The interesting point to note here is that Reich makes a distinction between three levels within the individual's psychology. At the highest and perhaps most superficial level is the one of everyday civil interaction, when human beings are not at each other's throats and are almost ritualistically polite to each other. Immediately below this surface calm, at an intermediate level, are the suppressed sexual anxieties and social uncertainties of individuals. It would be at this intermediate level that the collective mass psychology of fascism is likely to take hold, in Reich's analysis. At the lowest level of the very substrate of the human being, Reich seems to suggest that it is possible for individuals to be genuinely, as against superficially, considerate beings.[14] Here at this level they are capable of commendable acts of kindness, generosity and, dare one add, 'greatness'. As for instances of repetition ad nauseum of a country's greatness such as from Trump, it may be suggested that the greatest nations are likely to carry their greatness lightly rather than wear them on their sleeves or for that matter to conspicuously display them like some prefer to display their wealth.

The supposed attainment of the greatness of the nation is a project that is, more often than not, likely to fail. The next stage in the decline of democracy and the supposed simultaneous advance of greatness becomes the targeting of minority groups, who will be made scapegoats, the irritants and obstacles on whom can be heaped the blame for the nation's inability to achieve the much-cherished greatness. This follows from the spiral of inflammatory hatred and divisiveness which we have seen proliferate in democracies across the world. The point here is that these words do not remain inconsequential but become loose cannons in the body politic that can at any moment spark off a spiral of intense violence.

A threshold will somewhere and at some point be crossed that will signal the need to perpetrate intense violence against minorities. While there can be no predictable inevitability to the process, events in most democracies across the world are signalling a movement in which democracies in their present forms are serving as an instrument in the furtherance of hatred, rancour and eventual violence. This does not necessarily have to culminate in massacres and pogroms. However, the worsening international situation at present does not provide any sense of reassurance in terms of being able to counter such mass violence within nations.

After mass pogroms, massacres and instances of genocide, good-minded people are often known to assert that such atrocities should never happen again. One cannot doubt the goodness and genuineness of intention of such people. The problem is that available indicators are pointing towards the build-up of another round of violence across democracies in the world, where the state, rather than playing the role of a fair actor that prevents atrocities, will likely be employed in the actual perpetration of violence. The United Nations and other international organizations have often drawn up a list of early warning indicators. Again, a look at these early warning indicators and developments in many major democracies, including and especially India, provide little room for optimism. Reading a book such as the French historian and political scientist Jacques Semelin's *Purify and Destroy: The Political Uses of Massacre and Genocide* is disturbing as it suggests the dangers that many democracies are careening towards in their quest for purity and greatness.[15]

Appealing to the decency of Trump-like individuals is futile as there is no such element that exists there. However, there are good citizens, good men and women whose consciences will be troubled by the worsening hatred across the world stoked by politicians. Much hinges on them. If they speak up and condemn this, much good is likely to come out of such condemnation. It could even prevent the outbreak of violence. Keeping quiet, as many people are likely to do, will be a craven acquiescence to what Hannah Arendt famously referred to as the 'banality of evil'.[16]

Bearing Witness: Living in Times of Hate[1]

Navsharan Singh

In India, targeted violence is hardly new; the country's very birth as a modern nation state was accompanied by frenzied sectarian violence of unprecedented nature. The country responded by committing itself to a constitutional system focused on justice, liberty, equality and fraternity. The right to equality of all citizens ensured that no citizen was discriminated against by the state on the grounds of caste, sex, religion, race or colour; the right to freedom of religion was a natural corollary to this concept. The new nation committed itself to build on a normative idea which seeks to realize a secular society, one devoid of either inter-religious or intra-religious domination.

Within a few years, though, the normative ideal appeared to unravel. Starting as early as in 1961, when Jabalpur in Madhya Pradesh was rocked by major-scale violence between Hindus and Muslims, the history of post-Partition India is thickly dotted with violent episodes when people were targeted for their religious identity as the state machinery looked on in inaction or actively colluded with the perpetrators. From Bengali Muslims in Assam to Sikhs in Delhi, Muslims in Meerut, Bhagalpur, Gujarat and Muzaffarpur, Christians in Karnataka and Odisha, the history of targeted hate violence against minorities is not entirely new to India.[2]

However, something changed with the rise to dominance of the BJP, and especially since 2014 when the BJP and its allies formed the government at the Centre. The social and political landscape transformed to make way for the emergence of a majoritarian, hypernationalist state, brazenly committed to a Hindu *rashtra* and a relentless Hinduization of the public sphere.

According to the hate-crime tracker, an initiative led by IndiaSpend,[3] it was found that from 2009 to 2018, almost 90 per cent of religion-based crimes have occurred post the BJP taking power in 2014.[4] Hate crimes have now acquired a peculiar form of violence—'lynching', a frenzied attack allegedly by mobs on people mainly because of their religious identity. Lynch mobs have appeared across the landscape, killing Muslims and lower-caste Dalits suspected of slaughtering cows, and hate violence has been rising.

The murderous assault on Mohammad Akhlaque on 28 September 2015 in Dadri, Uttar Pradesh, was only a link in a long and grisly chain of killings in the name of the cow, with one person lynched every few days. Though Akhlaque's lynching[5] was reported widely, earlier in the same year, on 23 May, in Damoh, Madhya Pradesh,[6] two men were killed for transporting cows for slaughter; on 30 May, Abdul Ghaffar Qureshi[7] was lynched in Birloka, Rajasthan, by a mob on the suspicion that he *might*, in the future, sell beef; on 2 August, in Kaimrala, Uttar Pradesh, three alleged cattle thieves—Anaf, Arif and Nazim[8]—were lynched to death by a cow vigilante group; on 29 August, in Chilla village,[9] Delhi, vigilante groups attacked a truck carrying cattle allegedly for slaughter and badly injured the driver and others. What perhaps changed with Akhlaque was that he was lynched in his own home by people belonging to his own village. It was his fellow villagers who entered his home, and in the full presence of his family, attacked Akhlaque with sticks, bricks and knives, on the suspicion that he had stolen and slaughtered a cow calf and stored the meat in his fridge.

While Akhlaque's killing—and the images of his vandalized house, his coagulated blood on the floor, the petrified family, and the news of his younger son battling for life—shocked many, an uninterrupted cycle of violence was gradually congealing into a routine. In 2015, thirteen violent cow-related incidents, which claimed eleven lives, were recorded.[10]

The attacks continued the next year—each turning more gruesome than the other.[11] The incidents of cow-related attacks increased to thirty in 2016 and further to forty-three in 2017 and thirty-one in 2018. From 2009 till date, 127 incidents of vigilante attacks and forty-seven deaths have been recorded in cow-related violence.[12] The IndiaSpend hate crimes database, which records crimes motivated by religious hatred, documented 287 incidents of hate violence with ninety-eight deaths over the period 2009–19, with a majority of incidents recorded post-2014.[13]

The south and the east, which had seemed out of the Hindu nationalists' influence earlier, have joined the mainstream of hate. A certain everydayness has been imparted to these killings. Akhlaque was killed in his own home in Uttar Pradesh, Pehlu Khan on a busy road in broad daylight in Rajasthan, Junaid[14] in a crowded train in the National Capital Region, Delhi, Riyazuddin Ali and Abu Hanifa[15] at a farm near their home in Nagaon, Assam, Mazloom and Imtiaz Khan[16] killed and hung near their village in the small hours in Latehar, Abdul Basheer[17] brutally lynched to death in Mangaluru, and so on. A message is being writ large: you are not safe anywhere in the country. At the lynching sites, the victims are seen reduced to complete powerlessness, stripped of dignity, curled up, begging for water. Their condition seems to buoy up the perpetrators to hate them even more, and as the videos of the incidents circulate far and wide, other absent supporters partake in it vicariously.

Karwan-e-Mohabbat

As a response to this growing culture of violence and the impunity it enjoyed, in the summer of 2017, Harsh Mander, a civil rights activist, gave a call to form Karwan-e-Mohabbat, 'a journey of atonement, solidarity, and justice for people who had been targets of hate attacks across the country'.[18] For nearly two and a half years now, Karwan-e-Mohabbat has been visiting the families of victims of hate violence across India. Beginning in July 2017, it has concluded thirty-four journeys, traversing sixteen states. The journeys are helping to build a public archive of surviving in the times of hate.

Visiting with the families, the Karwan campaign listens to the survivors of hate violence and their families as they speak about the violence they endured, rebuilding lives, their long-drawn, and often seemingly impossible, battle for justice, their scramble for sheer survival. Families opened up, some reluctant initially, fearful and uncertain if they could trust us. Badly scarred by their experiences of violence and humiliation, they narrated their stories slowly and helped us make sense of almost a proxy war against Muslims in the country. It is not only the moment of violence but also the situation that ensues afterwards, that is one of dislocation and incoherence. The old claims to community, land, country lay in shambles: 'We had no animosity in the village',[19] 'We always celebrated Eid and Diwali together',[20] 'My son has Hindu friends who come home',[21] 'Our ancestors are buried on this land'.[22] This was a litany we heard everywhere.

And then: 'We love this country, we have the tricolour atop our house',[23] 'We stayed in India out of choice, not chance'. This was repeated over and over again, to proffer proof of their loyalty to the nation.

We witnessed the complete isolation of the families: 'No one from the Hindu families in the village came to mourn with us',

'They looked on as we prepared for *janaza*' (funeral prayer), 'We couldn't protect our own family from the attackers and the police never came',[24] 'Only jamaat came to help, we have no one else'.[25] As their access to the needed public, legal and institutional avenues shrink, as they experience the ruthless high-handedness of the police, the medical system and the courts, the families are pushed to take refuge in their own community and familial relationships. The citizens' fraternity is betrayed. They are reduced from citizens to a community.

The farmers in Mewat explained how their livelihoods were targeted systematically. They first lost their major source of income when mining was banned in the region, and cases were registered against drivers of vehicles used in mining, who were mostly Muslim youth. Next came under vicious attack their other principal source of income: dairy and cattle trade. 'We always kept cows and who says Muslims cannot keep cows in this country?' they asked.[26] 'If such is the belief, why not pass a law in the country that Muslims are not allowed to keep cows, why criminalize us?' they asked.[27] These are Muslim working-class people who live in the most economically and socially backward districts, hidden from policy and deprived of development.

The injustices heaped on them were not restricted to killing and maiming or confiscating their animals and ruining livelihoods; the police made regular rounds of their settlements and openly threatened them.[28]

They told us that they did not register FIRs against their losses because they feared counter-FIRs, which the police was successfully using across the country to shut the door of formal grievance redressal on them. Many mentioned how police filed complaints against the assault victims, their relatives and associates under laws banning cow slaughter. They said they did not steal cattle, it was farmers who sell their unproductive cow, bull or bullock, 'but we are made to feel like criminals'.[29]

The bereaved families were often in a state of incoherent dread and despair. Making sense of the 'madness' is not easy. 'Why did they do this to him? He was a very kind man,' said the wife of a brutally lynched man as she remembered him, confined to a small room without a view, completing her *iddat* (waiting) period.[30] Her husband, Qasim, used to buy young goats, fatten them at home and sell them after a few months for a small margin. He was too poor to trade in cows but he was lynched on the suspicion of carrying cows for slaughter.[31]

We witnessed families in isolation, retreating deeper into their shells, pushing the womenfolk further into the darker nooks of the private sphere, as they all struggled to deal with the consequences of hate violence and state apathy. We met women who were married off to very young brothers-in-law when the husbands were lynched by the mobs or killed in police encounters. We met them in their interior chambers as they grieved in isolation with no sororal support from the outside.

Some of these women were not just witnesses to the violence visited upon their male kin but were themselves assaulted in their own homes. But they were never called upon by inquiry officers, their statements never recorded, and injuries and insults never documented. When we, the women from Karwan, sat with them in their homes, there were long spells of quiet, and when they spoke, it was slowly, painfully, often in broken sentences, as though mustering words with all their strength. It was perhaps not the lack of words or an absent will to speak, but the *standing* to do so. How do they speak? Who listens to them? The customary practices assert that women's testimony is worthless, untrustworthy. But their testimony is blocked also in the practice of state institutions. They are non-citizens twice over. 'The mob entered our house, dragged and hit us as we begged to be spared.' They bared their bruised bodies as they said, 'Our bodies are still black and blue, but no one saw our scars.'[32]

We saw families in a state of utter despair. They were invariably poor, working class, with not much social capital, and not much capacity to fight back, or to sustain any legal battle for justice. They were often totally dependent on the small efforts and charity of the religious community to somehow survive in the wake of total destruction.

The lynching cases are often understood as spontaneous reactions of the mob. But the Karwan journeys exposed us to quite the opposite. The perpetrators shared an ideological orientation, chanted the same slogans, and often communicated through WhatsApp groups they were part of. This was no mob lynching—which assumes a modicum of spontaneity—but from the cases we visited, they appeared targeted, systematic, synchronized and organized attacks. In most states, the cow vigilante groups and the police function in a synchronized manner with a perfect division of labour. The vigilante group reports, the police intercept, the mob carries out the action as the police look on. 'We were called by a Hindu farmer who always sold his unproductive cattle to us. My father and I went and put the cattle in our pick-up van. It was a trap. Moments later, we hit the police barricade and the marauding mobs. My father asked me to run and save my life. I left the truck and ran. My father, too old to run, was lynched by the mob.'[33] This story was a testimony from Karnataka but it was repeated in Haryana and in western Uttar Pradesh, only the victims changed. 'An announcement was made from the local temple mic that a Muslim man was taking a cow for slaughtering and they should collect at the back of the temple,' villagers in Pelkhuwa told us, pointing to the temple some fifty yards away as we stood in the field looking at the blood-soaked mud, Qasim from the same village was attacked and killed at that spot. Qasim's rubber chappal still lay there with lumps of blood-soaked clay. We visited the place three days after the killing; the police had collected no samples, they told us, nor was the area cordoned off, we saw. 'When we showed the police the blood-soaked mud, they kicked and overturned the soil and asked us go away,' members of Qasim's family told us.

How the majoritarian political agenda is anti-poor and anti-labour is apparent from the vilification and violent attacks against those small self-employed people running abattoirs, dairies, small eateries, cattle trade, the migrants and the nomads. What is under attack here are the most fundamental of rights: to work and follow an occupation of one's choice, the right to worship, the right to travel without fear, and ultimately, the right to life.

Politics of Policymaking

In these journeys, even when we did not begin by a formal desire to do so, we perforce gathered 'data', and the testimonies, accounts of everyday violence, and patterns started to become visible. In our conversations with a range of people, we encountered an unrelenting Hindu nationalist surge and its normalization, and how it has seeped into policymaking.

Policies and state regulations have now been activated in support of the majoritarian agenda—the prohibition on selling cattle for non-agricultural purposes is being enforced, and there is mobilization of the Gau Raksha Dal (GRD) in Haryana, Uttar Pradesh, Rajasthan, Himachal Pradesh, Maharashtra, Goa, and Delhi. We witnessed the mechanics and use of public institutions in the service of the Hindutva project. We saw the modes of control, which were not limited to a general social, cultural dominance, but expanded to socio-economic dominance, and the use of policy for this dominance.

We learnt through the discussions in the villages how the new policy of cattle trade targeted both Muslim and Dalits to break their economic backs. On 23 May 2017 the Union Ministry of Environment, Forest and Climate Change notified the Prevention of Cruelty to Animals (Regulation of Livestock Markets) Rules, 2017, under the parent act, the Prevention of Cruelty to Animals Act, 1960, which effectively banned the sale of cattle in animal markets for purposes other than agricultural ones.[34] These rules laid an all-encompassing ban on the sale of animals, especially all bovine species including the buffalo, for the purpose of slaughter at animal fairs, and had far-reaching consequences impacting several industries—meat, leather, food and transport, which are populated mostly by Muslims and Dalits. Though regulating cattle trade is a state subject, animal welfare is overseen by the Centre. So, the environment ministry notified the rules under the animal welfare law and gave district administrations the power to enforce them. This led to the emergence of a complex web of state and non-state groups which enforce the larger design and the policy.[35] In Haryana, for example, the Gau Seva Aayog consists of twelve official members and twelve non-official members, including the chairman and the vice chairman.[36] The chairman is the head of the Aayog and presides over all the meetings of the Aayog. The chairperson and all members of the Aayog draw big salaries and allowances.[37] The secretary works as the chief executive officer of the Aayog and functions under the chairman of the Aayog. The Haryana government appointed a chief cow activist in the BJP-led cow protection cell, Gau Vansh Vikas Parokshth,[38] as the chairman of Haryana Gau Seva Aayog, and eleven other non-official members to the Aayog. Later an Indian Police Service (IPS) officer took charge as the CEO of the Gau Seva Aayog.[39]

The mandate of the Aayog is to work for the implementation of laws with respect to the prohibition of slaughter, and the welfare of cows, supervise the work of the institutions in relation to the scientific use of cow dung and urine, provide financial assistance to deserving institutions which are engaged in the welfare of cows, make people aware about the economic benefits of cows and arrange competitions to promote such awareness. The Aayog also took it upon itself to prepare a list of gau rakshaks in the state and issue identity cards to them. The gau rakshaks, who were until then private vigilantes, were to turn into bonafide agents of the state, with identity cards. This practice is not limited to Haryana; Maharashtra and Uttarakhand too have issued gau rakshaks identity cards.

These laws and regulations feed on and into a cultural discourse that constructs India as principally Hindu. The cow has emerged as the principal symbol and vehicle to create a consensus around India as primarily Hindu. These policies regarding the Gau Seva Aayog along with a complex web of rules and regulations, and vigilante violence are invoked to serve this purpose. Through this policy process, the Sangh organizations have successfully targeted and isolated a community while at the same time building a larger consensus for the Hindutva project. The Muslim is turned into a natural object of Hindu hate and a second-class citizen, too afraid to launch an FIR, approach a court, seek an apology or even grieve publicly or talk to strangers about their loss: '*Hamne sabr kar liya*' (We endured) was a phrase we heard time and again during our many interactions with aggrieved Muslim families across the country.

How Did We Get Here?

There has been no change in the language of the Constitution, despite threats from time to time by those whom the media designates as 'the fringe' that the Constitution shall be abandoned, or amended soon. And yet without having to change it, the idea of a secular republic has been severely strained as it constructs second-class citizenship for Muslims. Is it any surprise that their killers are defended, garlanded and offered tickets to contest elections?[40]

There has emerged a new consensus, and the edifice of constitutional guarantees of equality seems to be crumbling. At an election rally in Wardha on 1 April 2019, the crowd cheered as the country's prime minister thundered, 'Who attempted to defame our 5000-year-old culture? Who brought the word Hindu terrorism? Who committed the sin of labelling Hindus as terrorists?'[41] Again, in a post-2019 victory speech, the prime minister roared, 'For thirty years, there was a drama going on, there was a tag which was in fashion, wearing which all sins would be washed away. That fake tag was called secularism. But you would have witnessed that from 2014–19, a whole bunch stopped speaking . . . In this election not a single political party could dare to mislead the country by wearing the mask of secularism.'[42]

In a single speech, the prime minister demolished secularism and, in one stroke, he delegitimized the constitutional value of equality of religions. He conveyed that for the new state, Hinduism is not like any other religion, it is not cut from the same cloth, it is above all religions. Any association of Hindu outfits with violence was not only not conceivable, it was not acceptable. Similarly, by brandishing secularism as a fake claim, a pseudo philosophy, violence against Muslims is legitimized. There is no restraint on open claims of 'Hinduism first' in this country. The brazenness with which majoritarianism is legitimized has made violence normal, leading to a massive increase in hate crimes on the streets. A unity of purpose exists between the state and the non-state, and this is where consensus is built without altering the Constitution.

Light at the End of This Tunnel?

The lynched victims are dead. An entire community is living in fear, and India is disgraced. Is there a remedy, or will the nation confess that it cannot protect its Muslims, and also Christians, Dalits and tribals? Are we even willing to abolish the lynching? Something which began as a stray incident is now encountered over and over again; the lynchings of Muslim men continue in spite of plea and protest. Where do we go from here? The circle of hate is ever expanding; targets are only growing with each episode—with Akhlaque it was Muslims, in Una it was Dalits, in Assam it is the 'immigrant', and then the poets, writers, lawyers, human rights defenders, and trade unionists. How are we to protect speech? If voices are muffled, who will speak up? Who will seek the truth—the truth of the lynchings?

Is appeal to law the only certain remedy? Surely, we expect the judiciary to act whenever unbridled lawlessness prevails. The doors of the Supreme Court were knocked on, and on 17 July 2018, in the case of *Tehseen S. Poonawalla v. Union of India*,[43] a three-judge bench recognized the lynching and extrajudicial killings occurring as a result of cow vigilantism as unlawful. Recognizing the consequences of this targeted violence, the apex court then went on to issue a set of guidelines—preventive, remedial and punitive measures—to curb the widespread incidents of mob lynching in the country. From compulsory registration of first information reports (FIR), the appointment of a senior police officer as a nodal officer in each district for taking measures to prevent mob violence and lynching, the framing of a victim compensation scheme, a time-bound trial in the cases of mob lynching to departmental action against police or district officials who fail to act against the perpetrators. The Supreme Court also recommended that Parliament create a separate offence for lynching and provide adequate punishment for the same to 'instill a sense of fear for law amongst the people who involve themselves in such kinds of activities'. It has been one year since the Supreme Court's judgment, despite which increasing instances of lynchings continue to 'corrode the fabric of this nation'.[44]

Following the apex court guidelines, in July 2018 the central government constituted a high-level committee headed by the Union home secretary to suggest ways and means and a legal framework to effectively deal with incidents of mob lynching. The recommendation of the committee was to be considered by the group of ministers (GoM) headed by the Union home minister, which in turn would make a recommendation to the prime minister. While the committee prepared a report, the details have not been made public.[45]

Reports show that in multiple cases, even when the FIRs are registered, and the killers nabbed by the police, they are let off on bail. In the case of Junaid Khan, who was lynched in a crowded train, bail was granted to all the accused. In its order, the Punjab and Haryana High Court said that the initial dispute between the victims and the accused was 'only regarding the seat-sharing and abuses in the name of castes and nothing more'. The order said: 'There is neither any evidence of any preplanning to cause the incident deliberately or intentionally or to create disharmony.'[46] In the case of the Pehlu Khan lynching, the Rajasthan Police dropped the charges against all the six people he had named as accused in his dying declaration and an Alwar court permitted the Rajasthan Police to reinvestigate a case of cattle smuggling against the sons of Pehlu Khan, and reopen a charge sheet that had named Pehlu Khan.[47] In the case of Akhlaque's lynching, all the accused were granted bail. Convictions have been fewer and far between.

Similarly, compensation schemes for the families of victims suffer from the lack of uniformity. In Manipur, for instance, compensation is paid for death to the victim's next of kin, and calculated with the consideration of bodily, psychological and material injury. By contrast, Maharashtra sets compensation between two to three lakh or ten lakh in 'special cases'.[48] Given the variation of the schemes across states, in July 2019 the Supreme Court indicated that it would attempt to set further guidelines for a compensation scheme for victims of lynching.[49] Even in the debates in Parliament, the party in power dismissed the 'allegations' that impunity for lynchings is traced to their corridors.[50] In light of this and the tardy response by the states to the apex court's guidelines,[51] there is little hope that a new anti-lynching law will help the situation. It is the impunity which needs to be undone and the truth to be uncovered.

Lynching is openly mocking the law of the land and disgracing humanity. To undertake the work of making the 'law of the land' effective, perhaps a beginning in the right direction would be to seek a public inquiry into the incidents of lynching. This could take the form of a commission of inquiry with the participation of an influential body of citizens and jurists who oversee the investigation of each case and give the widest publicity to the facts in each case. In addition, for truth to be known, a detailed record of every lynching must be developed, a public record, and put out in the public domain so that the country knows the facts in each case. The National Crime Records Bureau (NCRB) does not maintain specific data with respect to the targeted incidents of violence in the country. It is important that this data be collected and put on record. Finally, in order to initiate the process through public inquiries, it will be imperative to take steps to build up public opinion as well as political action to deepen the movement to seek truth, justice and reparations for the victims of targeted violence.

Towards a New Equality Regime in India[1]

Farah Naqvi

Tales from the Everyday

Let us begin with stories, true and quotidian. An acquaintance who happens to be Dalit told me recently that he shifted from Noida to a rented house in south Delhi. It is closer to his workplace. The landlords are Mishras (Brahmins). The Dalit in question is a Valmiki with a disguised name. Years ago, he appended the catch-all 'Kumar' to his name in official papers. He does not discuss his identity with strangers (including potential landlords), and I have never quizzed him about his name. But what I do know is he may not get the apartment without it. A Muslim female colleague just rented an office space in one of Delhi's urban villages—Khirki. She paid more rent for it than the market value but is relieved that she got it at all. Her husband is Hindu, so the lease was in his Punjabi-Hindu name. She knows they paid more rent than a Hindu would, and more than the going market rate, but did not dare to bargain. We have all read stories about film actors with Muslim names in Mumbai facing hostility at the gates of housing societies.

Ten-odd years ago, a friend's son was in a Delhi preschool, which was voted by a leading education journal as 'the best preschool in India'. It decided to schedule its annual PTA on Eid-ul-Fitr (the 'big' Eid), a joyous celebration at the end of the month-long Ramadan fast. It is the biggest Muslim festival of the year, on par with Diwali for Hindus and Christmas for Christians. She went for the PTA but gently chided the principal and class teacher. The result—bewildered but profuse apologies and a phone call from the teacher a few days prior to the *other* Eid (Eid-ul-Zuha), which commemorates Abraham's sacrifice of his son Ismail to God. The teacher asked my friend if she would like to come to the school and share something special about Eid with her son's class. My friend, a busy professional, gently turned down the offer. Hours later, the principal called her, saying, 'You know, we just had Eid on 17 November, and now 17 December is Muharrum. Is that important to you? Because, you see, because of the Commonwealth Games we lost a lot of days, and there are only three children who observe this religion, and one of them is Pakistani and they are out of town anyway, and none of our teachers observe it, so I will speak to the one remaining parent if it is okay with you?' My friend was in fury. The same preschool had declared Karva Chauth a holiday because all the teachers were busy fasting. 'I would frankly rather declare Russian New Year a holiday—at least we used to like the Russians once,' she fumed. 'And I can give a damn good lecture about Diwali too, so why is it that a fancy preschool needs a "Muslim" to educate their toddlers about a festival important to 180 million Indians.' She ranted and raved, but did not escalate the matter. 'I don't want my three-and-a-half-year-old to be singled out as the one with the troublesome mum,' she said.

Muharrum is a gazetted holiday, and frankly, even if there isn't a single child who observes 'this religion', it must be declared a holiday as a matter of respectful policy, in keeping with the public culture of a secular state and in the interest of teaching respect for all religions to our young ones. You could say that I am overreacting. The preschool was, after all, being nice by asking my friend to come and share Eid stories, and asking her to give permission for them to keep the school open on Muharrum. But they were not. They were revealing the degree of 'othering' that exists in our society, the fear of discrimination that skulks just beneath the surface of the lives of those who do not conform to the cultural mainstream. School holidays on religious occasions are not a matter of personal favours between a parent and an institution; it is a social contract between public educational institutions and the ethos of the nation that they flourish in. In trying to make this a personal matter, the school (whether through ignorance or intent) violated that social contract. It discriminated.

African students in Delhi face racism, from physical violence to routine discrimination. Shopkeepers serve them last when they enter first, restaurants seat them at the worst tables even on empty days. An effeminate gay man did not get the job he qualified for because it was a front desk job, and the hotel owners felt their middle-class clientele would get put off by 'how he appeared'. The OBC aspirant with a Muslim name did not make it to the next round of a higher education fellowship awarded by a private foundation because someone on the interview panel preferred the more confident upper-caste Hindu boy.

Across a range of public services—from ration shops to public healthcare, from schools to employment (including Mahatma Gandhi National Rural Employment Guarantee Scheme [MGNREGS] job cards), in giving loans, in the allotment of homes, in colleges, parks, shops, hospitals, banks—discrimination can be felt in your bones.

Despite the equality mantras (Articles 14, 15, 16, 17, 21 . . .) enshrined in our Constitution, India remains a deeply stratified society. A quick glance at any matrimonial website will remind us that huge swathes of our population embrace the prejudice of ascriptive difference, with no apology or embarrassment. And it is not the grand diversity of equals. It is a hierarchical difference; some groups have greater social, economic and political power than others. Those higher in the pecking order exercise power, and control access to precious goods, services and resources needed by others. When they act on their personal prejudice based on ascriptive identities, they thwart equality every day. Those discriminated against—those lower down in the social pecking order, Dalits, Muslims, tribals, other minorities, the physically challenged, women, sexual minorities—are then actively prevented from partaking equally of the fruits of national development and national life, from accessing equal opportunities to better their lives.

Nations around the world, with far fewer endemic and deep-rooted discriminatory societal norms, often have more than a single anti-discrimination law and multiple mechanisms to protect against a range of discriminations, whether based on gender, race, ethnicity, sexuality, or age and marital status. In India, we have none—making us perhaps the only modern democracy without any statutory framework that recognizes discrimination. In most democratic jurisdictions, acts of discrimination are actionable. Civil cases can be filed, and until such time as people learn to keep their prejudices to themselves, there can be consequences and correctives. This has long remained a gap in Indian law, in our imagination of equality, and in our collective will to seriously dent inequity rather than simply manage it.

Beyond Quotas and Commissions

As a nation we appear to manage inequality without denting it, manage it the same way we manage corruption—a sop here and a mop there. But the cesspool remains as putrid and the bias as deep. Inequity management systems in India have grown old but strong, and spread roots deep in the ground.

We manage inequality in group-based silos of protectionism. What have been our dominant inequity management strategies? Quotas, commissions and ministries. Reserved quotas for Dalits and Adivasis were constitutionally sanctioned—22.5 per cent seats in public sector jobs, educational institutions and legislatures.

Since then, we have expanded it to include 27 per cent quotas for OBCs in public sector jobs and higher education, and in some states a handful of Muslims have sneaked in through inclusion in other quota categories. Despite a 50 per cent Supreme Court cap on quotas, several states flout this diktat. The 1995 Disability Act gave a 3 per cent quota to the disabled in government jobs, much of which remains unfilled. The seventy-third and seventy-fourth constitutional amendments in 1992 gave women 33 per cent seats in panchayati raj bodies.

While there is no denying that quotas have made a critical difference in denting the stranglehold of caste-based inequities, quotas are being strongly resisted in the private sector, and Dalits still have a hard time getting loans and finding homes to rent. Despite the Scheduled Castes (SCs) and Scheduled Tribes (STs) (Prevention of Atrocities) Act, unspeakable violence as well as everyday forms of discrimination against Dalits are a daily occurrence across the country. There is continued anger and a sense of disenfranchisement among Dalits. Quotas have not meant the end of daily discrimination.

Proliferating group-specific ministries is the other way we seek to address group-specific deprivation. The Ministry of Social Justice and Empowerment (MoSJE) was bifurcated in 1999 to create the Ministry of Tribal Affairs. And then further lost another 'group' (the minorities)[2] to the Ministry of Minority Affairs, set up in 2006. So MoSJE now does policy, planning and coordination of programmes for the development of SCs, OBCs and the disabled. For women, there is the Ministry of Women and Child Development.

Ministries are useful in targeting and making visible allocation of resources, and developing programmes to address group-specific inequity. Mere resource allocation does not, however, correct for bias and prejudice in implementation at lower levels, which is generally where the problem lies. Besides, and this concern was voiced even in 2006 when the Ministry of Minority Affairs was born, it does create yet another 'separate' and competing strand in our overall inequity management system. Ministries obviously compete for limited resources for *their* group.

From the 1990s we have also inaugurated an era of group-specific commissions to further our stated equity agenda.[3] Each commission is managed by the various group-specific ministries mentioned above.[4] Barring the National Commission for Backward Classes (NCBC) (which chiefly examines inclusion and exclusion of citizens from the central list of socially and educationally backward classes), the other group-specific commissions have a broad-based mandate to promote welfare and equity. Some have individual complaints mechanisms, but armed with little other than recommendatory and advisory powers, they have been less than useful.

Successive governments have treated these commissions shamefully, failing to table and debate their reports in Parliament, or take on board their recommendations, and systematically eroded their autonomy by using them as parking lots for party loyalists who have to be accommodated somewhere. These are not solutions to inequity.

What can get us out of this culture of a zero-sum game? Of dividing the pie, of turf battles for equity among the perpetual unequals? Quotas for the historically deprived *must* be supported, for they provide tangible, assured inclusion. But quotas are by definition a zero-sum game. If there are 100 places, there are only a few limited ways these can be divided. *Other equality solutions must be allowed to emerge.* The group-specific commissions have clearly proved less than useful in battling the myriad forms of discrimination that pervade our system and society.

How do we begin to create a unifying lateral movement between various deprived groups? How do we begin to find common ground, and create integrated pressure on an unresponsive system for more equitable distribution of goods and services, rather than remain mired in separate strands of inequity management?

An Equal Opportunity Commission for All

In 2006, when the Sachar Committee report (on the social, economic and educational status of Muslims) came out, the million-dollar question doing the rounds was 'Will they recommend quotas?' Of course they did not. They could not. The nation was repeatedly told that there was no constitutional sanction for reservations based on religious community. While many believe the argument is morally flawed (and in the face of acute deprivation of Muslims, the Constitution can be amended, as it has been hundreds of times), that is a debate for another article. The Sachar Committee, unable to arrive at the easy quota solution, was forced to think out of the box. It emerged with one idea that represents a vital discursive shift—an EOC: 'The Committee recommends that an Equal Opportunity Commission should be constituted by the government to look into the grievances of the deprived groups.'[5]

The idea cut across the separate silos of competitive inequity claims, carrying within it kernels of a new equality regime in India. The EOC recommendation of Sachar was pointedly for *all* 'deprived groups', not just Muslims.

In 2008, an expert group set up by the Ministry of Minority Affairs (headed by legal expert late Prof. N.R. Madhava Menon) developed the EOC idea into an implementation model, including a legislative framework.[6] And President Pratibha Patil's speech of 4 June 2009 committed UPA-II to setting it up.[7]

Unfortunately, the EOC bill proposed by the Menon Committee, while good in principle, was weak in detail. It essentially proposed a host of research, advisory and advocacy functions and a 'group complaints' model, while failing to provide effective remedies for individual discrimination complaints. It spoke only of education and employment as sectors to be covered, whereas we need anti-discrimination measures in several arenas—housing, delivery of schemes, public services, as well as in the private sector and covering private bodies.

An EOC without Anti-Discrimination Law: Cart before Horse?

The proposed EOC was also a bit 'cart before horse', in that the bill did not state anywhere that 'discrimination is illegal'. It merely cited the constitutional promises of equality, and said that there is no need to restate the obvious, that is, to *explicitly prohibit discrimination*. What the Menon report failed to note was that the constitutional prohibition of discrimination covers only state actions, not the private sector. And that is just not good enough.

Besides, the Constitution provides vision. For citizens to activate it, bring it to life, we need to give it legislative teeth, in the form of a *comprehensive anti-discrimination law*. An EOC can then implement the provisions of such a law through legal definitions, clear rules and procedures. What is the definition of discrimination, victimization or harassment? What will be the standard of proof in individual cases? How will we tackle group discrimination? What will be the remedy across a range of sectors?

Such a law may help the existing national commissions that attempt dispute resolution, and handle individual complaints of discrimination. Because notions of 'discrimination' and 'equal opportunity' are clearly stated in our Constitution,[8] the group-specific commissions, mandated to promote equality within a constitutional framework, have been handling cases of discrimination for years together but without any definitional clarity or guidelines—all ad hoc, arbitrary.

For example, during 2017–18, the Complaints and Investigation Cell of the National Commission for Women (NCW) registered 15,381 complaints/cases falling within its mandate.[9] These related to a range of issues—bigamy/polygamy, cyber crime, dowry harassment/dowry death, free legal aid for women, police apathy, and many other violations. But, notably, also related to the 'right to live with dignity' and 'gender discrimination including equal right to education, and in work'.[10] In the same year, the National

Commission for Minorities (NCM) recorded 1498 complaints.[11] The National Commission for Scheduled Castes (NCSC) handled far greater numbers.

The point is that these thousands of complaints, bespeaking huge inequity, have failed to add up to a coherent body of understanding of how the average Indian citizen experiences a range of discriminatory practices. Or how we as a nation can collectively address discrimination. This is chiefly because these complaints are handled in separate silos of various commissions, and in the absence of a common legal, definitional and procedural framework, they have only led to ad hoc remedies. So we have no idea how the NCW, NCM or NCSC even define 'discrimination', or what kinds of relief they propose as they 'dispose of' these complaints. Only a comprehensive anti-discrimination law can provide that legal coherence.

Turf Wars: Will an EOC Weaken Our Existing Commissions?

Histories of policymaking are instructive, because they warn of the pitfalls ahead. In 2010, even as the public debate on the EOC had barely begun, and the idea of an anti-discrimination law hadn't even taken off, the institutional turf wars began.

UPA-II set up a GoM to examine the proposal. And before the EOC could take flight, it was quickly swatted down by competing claims and turf wars that our inequity management systems have spawned. A close look at the GoM is revealing. The GoM, headed by A.K. Antony, and comprising a host of ministers, decided that an EOC should be set up only for 'minorities' (a euphemism for Muslims). This was an alarming twist in the tale.[12] Why would such a preposterous recommendation be made? After all, the framework of the EOC being proposed spoke of equal opportunity measures for *all* deprived groups in both public and private sectors (which has resisted quotas).

And yet a host of Dalit and tribal leaders from within the Congress—Mukul Wasnik, Kantilal Bhuria and Mallikarjun Kharge—pushed for a 'truncated EOC' (that is, only for minorities). And, in support, the then Union tourism minister, Selja Kumari, and the women and child development minister, Krishna Tirath, both Dalit faces of the Congress, warned that the GoM's decision 'should not dilute the powers of SC/ST commissions'! Other GoM members (Montek Singh Ahluwalia, Kapil Sibal and P. Chidambaram) supported this absurd idea—an EOC *only* for minorities. Salman Khurshid, who (along with Veerappa Moily) was arguing for an inclusive EOC to cover all deprived groups, was left, quite literally, in the minority.[13]

It seemed clear that those who speak on behalf of groups that have quotas in government jobs don't find the EOC idea tempting enough. On the one hand is secure inclusion through quotas, on the other, the uncertain outcome of an EOC that will 'attempt to stop discrimination' in the private sector. This was coupled with the fear that an idea like the EOC will gradually weaken the overall edifice of inequity management and will entail serious turf encroachment—taking away functions from the myriad group-specific commissions.

But we all know that an EOC for minorities *alone* can never fly. It will lead to charges of appeasement from the right, and to anger from all groups (including SCs/STs) who are denied its benefits. At best, it will be allowed to develop into yet another weak, ghettoized little body talking only to itself.

These battles are an indicator of just how entrenched our inequity management politics is, and how bumpy the ride ahead is likely to be. Yet it is a journey we must embark upon. The experience of the United Kingdom may be useful here. In Great Britain, over the years there have been different statutory bodies that dealt with specific aspects of discrimination. The Equal Opportunities Commission was established to tackle the issue of sex discrimination. The Disability Rights Commission focused on issues related to disability discrimination, and the Commission for Racial Equality dealt with race discrimination. In October 2007, these three commissions were merged into the new body called the Equality and Human Rights Commission (EHRC). In addition to taking on the responsibilities of the three existing commissions, the EHRC also acquired new responsibilities in order to cover many additional strands of discrimination.

Also, through an Act of Parliament, the UK brought in the Equality Act, 2010. Before this, the UK had several acts and regulations that formed a broad anti-discrimination regime. The Equality Act merged nine main pieces of legislation: the Equal Pay Act, 1970; the Sex Discrimination Act, 1975; the Race Relations Act, 1976; the Disability Discrimination Act, 1995; the Employment Equality (Religion or Belief) Regulations, 2003; the Employment Equality (Sexual Orientation) Regulations, 2003; the Employment Equality (Age) Regulations, 2006; the Equality Act, 2006, Part 2, and the Equality Act (Sexual Orientation) Regulations, 2007.

The new Equality Act, 2010, now protects people against discrimination, harassment or victimization in employment, and as users of private and public services based on nine protected characteristics: age, disability, gender reassignment, marriage and civil partnership, pregnancy and maternity, race, religion or belief, sex, and sexual orientation.

These mergers were not easy. It took political wrangling, institutional foot-dragging, ideological debates, and yet the logic of coherence won. And the hope of a better equality regime did finally make it happen. Legal models can never be transplanted from one country or one jurisdiction to another. This example is merely to say that India can find its own path to a harmonious, simple, comprehensible equality regime for all its citizens.

Towards a New Equality Regime for *All*

It is absurd that in a country like India, where identity-based discrimination is the norm rather than the exception, we have only now woken up to even discussing broad anti-discrimination legislation. Even for our constitutionally acknowledged 'deprived' groups (SCs/STs), we have only managed the SC and ST (Prevention of Atrocities) Act, 1989, which provides *no* remedies for insidious daily discrimination. We have limited our imagination to quotas and commissions. And it is time to break the impasse.

What we need to talk about is a whole series of affirmative action interventions, an enabling environment, back-end subsidies to institutions that promote weaker sections, codes of conduct, and anti-discrimination legislation (covering both public and private sectors) that precede the formation of an EOC. We also need to think of rationalizing the roles and functions of other national commissions and evolve clarity on the institutional relationship between them and a future unified EOC.

An anti-discrimination regime with a civil legislation and an EOC to implement it can cut across silos of protectionism that mark our inequity management strategies. It can push us into an era of denting inequity instead of just managing it. We cannot legislate against bias in the hearts and minds of people, but we can legislate against bias, prejudice and discrimination in how the fruits of national development and opportunity are distributed among our citizens. Let us inaugurate an equality regime that does not weaken reservations/quotas or existing commissions, but allows our imagination to go beyond them. Let us seek common ground for all deprived sections, rather than perpetuating inequity through management systems of isolated, competing silos, always separate and always unequal.

Minorities, Market and Accumulation[1]

Barbara Harriss-White

In India, while an extensive body of universalistic laws, which are rationalist in spirit, has been created to regulate the economy, its implementation is far from being universal, its rationale is heavily contested and its practice instituted through local power structures. Equality of citizenship is also actively contested—notably by propertied, high-status men. Regulation on the ground is shaped by local interests, particularly those of India's numerous intermediate class. So it is reasonable to ask whether, and if so, how, religions may shape regulative practice, in the same way that caste does in some parts of India.

While the history of the relation between religion, politics and the construction of the nation is well established, the relationship between India's religions, the market economy and the process of accumulation is strikingly under-researched. This essay is a journey of reconnaissance into the ways in which religions structure Indian capitalism, looking especially at the case of minorities, and focusing on the informal economy, that remains for the most part out of the direct reach of the state.

Muslims

India has more Muslims than any other nation except for Indonesia—172 million in 2011, making up 14.2 per cent of the population.[2] Their uneven dispersal affects the many roles they play in the economy. Half of India's Muslims are compacted into the northern 'Hindi heartland' and West Bengal. There are smaller concentrations in peninsular India, on the Kerala coast and by the border with Pakistan. While most Muslims live in rural areas, they are nonetheless twice as urbanized as their population share would suggest.[3]

'Difference' has been codified in laws grounded in religion; electoral democracy evolved to cater separately for electorates defined in terms of their religions, and the history of modern India has been punctuated by eruptions of violence between Hindus and Muslims. But Muslims are not covered by India's laws of positive discrimination. And while Hindu nationalists have depicted an Islamic 'community' as both threatening and indulged, if there is a 'problem' of Muslims in the Indian economy then it is one of human underdevelopment, economic backwardness and underperformance rather than one of superior economic power.[4]

Although Muslims are disproportionately urban, they are extremely under-represented in India's capitalist elite, as well as in the Indian state apparatus. At the same time, the population of Muslims is highly differentiated in complex ways—according to sect, to internal, caste-like stratification, to *biradari* (industrial/occupational guilds) and region. Upon this cultural and religious differentiation, their equally complex economic differentiation has to be mapped. The first element in this differentiation is the Muslim peasantry, most heavily concentrated in Jammu and Kashmir and the Ganges Valley belt along the southern border with Nepal. While this peasantry is itself internally differentiated by landholding, operational scale and labour process, two features stand out. First, the mass of Muslim cultivators are small peasants in regions of poor irrigation—which have lagged in the adoption of new agricultural technology—and in agrarian structures where strong elements of extra-economic compulsion persist.

Second, throughout India, as of 2009–10, while the proportion of the rural Muslim workforce engaged in agricultural labour (23 per cent) is less than that of rural Hindus (26 per cent), Muslims self-employed in agriculture (21 per cent) are far fewer than Hindus (33 per cent). Muslims also have a 25 per cent higher incidence of landlessness, and the proportion of rural Muslims in non-agricultural wage work, artisanal craft production and what is still known as 'menial work' (services and petty trade, much of which involves high levels of skill but low levels of pay) is also greater—25 per cent contrasted with 15 per cent of rural Hindus.[5]

On the one hand, the occupational distribution of rural Muslims in contemporary India shows a distinctive 'path dependence' from the Mughal era of courtly patronage and exploitation. On the other hand, their social separation from Hindus and their freedom from Hindus' distinctive social obligations may have encouraged innovative activity.

Another element in the economic differentiation of Muslims is the downward mobility resulting from the migration to Pakistan of professionals and the Ashrafi elite, and from the political degeneration of Islamic feudalism after Independence. In the wake of the state-enforced zamindari abolition in Uttar Pradesh and Hyderabad, the absentee landowning aristocracy and their retainers lost their role and, often, their livelihoods, dragging with them the urban and rural artisans whose livelihoods had depended on courtly tastes and demand. Only a small and educated minority of the landed elite remained near the seats of power and obtained employment and new status, often retaining control over their land through renting and letting.

The Case of Siliguri

These elements may be seen at work in Siliguri, a rapidly growing town of some 2,00,000 inhabitants, distributing consumption goods to the plantation region of West Bengal. While the territory of the future town had been owned entirely by powerful Muslim families, 'due to miscalculation, uneconomic habits and family litigation, these Muslim personalities lost their land, capital, power and position'[6] and at Partition they were forced to East Bengal. As Siliguri expanded, some 10,000 Muslims migrated there, establishing themselves mainly in slums alongside low-caste Hindus in a 'microcosm of Muslim society and culture'.[7] In Siliguri now, Muslim men work as traders, skilled artisans, recyclers and providers of petty services. Old links between biradari and occupation are dissolving; endogamous groups have become less rigid. Nevertheless, the occupations of tailoring, cotton carding, fishmongering, goat butchery, greengrocery and bookbinding are still carried out by Muslims in occupational groups. While alliances now blur the social boundaries of the Ashrafi elite and Ajlaf subordinates, new socio-economic categories with new economic meanings are being formed. These distinguish the *amir* (the educated, rich few) from the *garib* (the poor majority). Despite this internal economic and cultural differentiation, Muslims in Siliguri are generally described as being poor, socially separate, and marginalized by their religion and its impact on their education. Siliguri's Muslims, especially their girls, are relatively poorly educated. Muslim children are educated in separate religious schools (madrasas) and in Urdu rather than Bengali, the local language.[8]

Another major element in the economic positioning of Muslims is their tendency to occupy niches historically shunned by Hindus for reasons of ritual pollution. So butchers may be either untouchables, or Muslims—Qassabs. Muslim control of tanning, glue, soap, hides and leather (and rubber and plastic) shoes and other leather goods production (and now export) has developed from their important role in butchery. Small-town restaurants ('military hotels') have developed based on Muslim culinary specialities that include meat, as much as from Hindu rules of commensality, which long prevented all but the ritually purest from running even vegetarian eating places.

The Case of South Indian Leather

The case of the leather industry in Tamil Nadu, in south India, shows how a series of factors have transformed the way it had been stratified by religion, though it is still controlled by Muslims. At the macro level, state policy has required the export of hides to be replaced by semi-finished and finished leather products. At the micro level, the diffusion of demands for dowries from upper into the lower castes has changed Hindu social attitudes to work involving ritually polluting substances as bride-givers come under social compulsion to supply dowries. The production of leather goods is being vertically integrated, and the labour process is being transformed from one using casual workforces confined to Muslim or Scheduled Caste labourers working on-site to one that includes the subcontracting of stitching and other processes to poor, forward-caste child and female workers. They work at some distance from the tanneries, in the seclusion of their homes and in an atmosphere of 'shame' and of patriarchal compulsion.

The worldwide rise in demand for Indian leather products and the entrepreneurial responses to this by Muslim tanners have led to the rapid accumulation of considerable capital and to new portfolios of Muslim investment in agribusiness and property. Already in the 1970s, the acquisition of the trappings of high status by Muslims in the leather industry had 'begun to distort the traditional system of social stratification and rank order'.[9] In recent years, the increase in violence and lynching with impunity of Muslims (and Dalits) suspected or associated with the beef industry together with tougher laws on the slaughter and transport of beef has challenged Muslim wealth in beef and leather.[10] These developments have disrupted the livelihoods of farmers, herders, cattle transporters and traders, and the major businesses of beef and leather exports, disproportionately affecting Muslims.[11]

But the transformation of cattle into commodities has not been the only route to accumulation that ritually polluting niches in the economy have opened up for Muslims. The predominance of Muslims in bidi (country cigarette) production (where Muslims comprise 80 per cent of the workforce, though they own none of the dominant brands) is explained by both the caste Hindu's avoidance of pollution and by the fact that smoking was introduced into India by Muslims. Muslims also cite 'Hindu ritual pollution' as the reason for their control of the recycling of physically polluting waste and scrap: bone, paper, card, metal, glass and plastics. In many regions, Muslims dominate plumbing, masonry and metal products, hardware, locks and even mechanical and electrical repairs, which are thought to trace back to the conversion to Islam of low-caste Hindu *lohar* blacksmiths.[12]

Yet another element that has given Muslims a distinctive role in the economy is the revival and expansion of industries whose workforces require highly skilled craftsmen. Craft skills are reproduced in the families of artisans which survived the decline in the 1950s and 1960s of the princely patronage that had given them life. These families responded to the transformation of services and goods for a few patrons into the supply of commodities for national and international demand. As a result, many of the craft-based industries have remained strikingly localized. So in Uttar Pradesh, for example, Muslim artisans produce brassware in Moradabad, pottery in Khurja, glassware in Firozabad, carpets in Bhadohi and Mirzapur, carpentry and woodwork in Saharanpur, handprinted textiles in Farrukhabad, cotton and silk embroidery in Varanasi, perfume manufacturing (to which the development of Unani medicines is related) in Lucknow, Kannauj and Jaunpur and handloom cloth in Mau. In Bihar, large numbers of Muslims are silk and cotton handloom weavers. Muslim workers dominate the bidri-ware and carpet industries in Andhra Pradesh, and silkworm rearing and toy industries in Karnataka. In Jaipur, Rajasthan, some of the stonecutters and marble workers are Muslim (though tribal women and children are also used in quarrying), and Gujarat's block and screen printing industry employs Chippas, a Muslim group.

Certain of these craft-based industries have evolved into a full-blown local Muslim capitalism. The examples most often quoted are Moradabad brassware, which has profited from demand from the Middle East, and cloth and clothing manufacture and trade, which have developed from the skills of Muslim tailors (*darzis*) and weavers (*julahas*). It is quite common for the surplus in these industries to be appropriated from the Muslim workers by Hindu and Jain immigrant trading castes which proceed to reinvest it elsewhere. These traders routinely supply production and consumption credit and raw materials, and sometimes have been found to provide food as an advance against pay. They arrange sales, state licences, development permits, and finance and organize technical change.[13]

Given that in sectors where Muslims provide the uneducated but skilled labour force, and the traders are not necessarily Muslim, it has often been concluded that the 'Indian Muslim [has a] dislike for trade and commerce'.[14] More specifically it is said that 'the generality of Muslims in Hindustan and the Deccan kept away from trade and commerce, at least up until independence'[15] and even that they have been 'devoid of a middle class of businessmen' since then.[16] However, Mattison Mines's study of Muslim merchants in Pallavaram in northern Tamil Nadu, published in 1972, showed that while high-caste Hindus spurned commerce there, the conduct of business by Muslims was regarded as a *sunnath*, a custom of the Prophet's, and therefore as 'an occupation conveying religious merit'.[17]

The fact that these merchants were Muslim could not be separated from their being in a type of bazaar trade which was not regulated by the state. Nor could it be distinguished from the fact that it belonged to a particular place. The significance for accumulation of being Muslim was therefore ambiguous. The influence of Islam was expressed in a variety of ways, including a pronounced preference for the employment of Muslim wage labour by Muslim merchants—a spreading of opportunities for livelihood most easily achieved in the bazaar economy. Further, the universalist cosmopolitanism of Islam meant that there were trusted contacts at long distances, including overseas, ready to develop trade networks.[18] At the time of Mines's fieldwork, however, these 'bazaar' merchants had not expanded into national trade networks or industries—whether 'small-scale' (as the Muslim leather industry nearby was then classified) or corporate. This was attributed by Mines to the constraints of 'embeddedness' in the personalized and informalized bazaar economy. In the bazaar, while credit was available through established links of trust and mutual dependence, its scale was too small and too short-term for investment in industry. In the bazaar too, practical experience was valued above the technical education needed to manage industry. A family or kin-based workforce was still valued above cosmopolitan contractual relations.[19]

In the absence of other systematic evidence on the reach of Muslim business, Wright's analysis of advertisements over a run of fourteen years in *Radiance*, an English-language weekly magazine of the Jamaat-e-Islami, demonstrates that both upwardly mobile Ajlaf and downwardly mobile and adaptable Ashrafi capitalists formed a largely metropolitan body of Muslim accumulators. But Wright concluded: '[T]he trouble is that as the traditional functional division of labour between religious communities as well as sects and *jatis* breaks down . . . competition can and does erupt into politicised violence.'

This violence has only intensified since.

Christians

Considered the second largest minority here, Christians comprised only 2.3 per cent of the Indian population in 2011, though numbering a substantial 28 million. While a third of Goans are Christian, and while Christians form the majority in almost all the small states of the north-east, most Christians are to be found in

Kerala, where they account for 18 per cent of the total population, and in a belt in Tamil Nadu, where they account for 6 per cent. In half the states of India, Christians number fewer than 1 per cent and are mostly marginal peasants and agricultural labourers.[20] The history and geography of conversion has resulted in distinct and separate groupings and denominations, polarized at their extremes between Syrian Christians in Kerala on the one hand, who trace themselves back to Brahmins converted by the apostle Thomas (who arrived in India in 52 CE), and Dalit and tribal Christians on the other who converted in mass movements from the last part of the nineteenth century onwards.

Syrian Christians have developed as a 'jati among other jatis'.[21] They are said to live in relative social exclusivity to this day, perhaps because of—rather than despite—their having multiplied into no less than fifteen denominations, and their long history of accommodation with imperial power. Joining British capital as workers, supervisors and agents, they differentiated into money-dealing, industrial capital and commercial capitalism. From here, they moved on to establish credit institutions and modern banking on the one hand, and the rubber and tea plantations, the development of vertically integrated agribusiness (and the joint stock form of corporate ownership) on the other. Syrian Christians are now well represented in the state and in corporate sector management. But using tightly knit credit, Syrian Christians have also invaded low-status sectors. In Kerala and elsewhere, they dominate mechanized fishing, chains of beauty parlours and dry cleaning.

The Christian churches (particularly the Roman Catholic Church under the Portuguese) also accumulated significant capital assets and are now major employers in their own right. Tapping foreign aid and state subsidies too, churches run by high-caste Catholics have invested in educational and medical infrastructure, commercial property, farms and factories. Their surplus is ploughed back and also invested in India's capital markets. However, church institutions cannot possibly employ all the low-caste and Dalit Catholics who need work.[22]

When Dalits converted to Christianity, they were no longer eligible for state support under the system of educational and job reservations for Scheduled and other low ('backward') castes. Their livelihoods now depended on education and on wide regional networks of Christian contacts. So a minority of educated Christians 'became teachers, clerks, nurses, hospital attendants, railway and postal employees, drivers, conductors, mechanics and policemen. Some have become doctors, professors, advocates, writers, singers, printers and engineers and a few have become higher level government officials.'[23] Their descendants form an urban, propertied, educated, salaried and professional elite, some of whom have interests in rural land. The great majority, however, remain rural wage workers and 'in the highly competitive struggle for upward mobility they face prejudices both as Dalits and as Christians'.[24]

Caste, Christianity and Economic Change

David Mosse's study of a village in southern Tamil Nadu where a large Harijan (outcaste/Dalit) population is divided between Hindus and Christians, and further between Catholics and Protestants, shows that all the Harijan castes have been struggling to reduce the relations of subordination in which they are locked— through patronage, dependence on tenancy and many kinds of service provision.[25] Yet in an elaborate process of status mobility (involving 'downward displacement, role bifurcations and trade-offs between status and resources'), Christianity has helped people not only to reduce their economic relations of dependence (as in the case of Protestant Harijan Paraiyar caste) but also to achieve specific indicators of higher status (for instance, the Catholic Harijan Pallar caste).[26] People at the very bottom of the system of Harijan caste rankings provide services reciprocally or on a market basis, though market exchange is qualified by personalized transactions.

Elsewhere, contracts are reworked in the idioms of higher status. Instead of work on order, there is negotiation, with honorific presentations, cash payment and the development of new contexts in which services can be provided and received. Demeaning tasks and forms of payment are transferred to women or avoided through migration. Markets for credit and labour have been created, and the principle that Christian Harijan Pallars can have rights to private landownership has been established. Mosse finds that 'religion makes no difference to [the] inter caste relations' of hierarchy and rank being replicated and challenged by Harijans.[27]

Each episode of assertion has been organized at the level of the individual economic service performed. The history of emancipation for cattle scavengers is different from that for the operators of irrigation sluices; the history of Catholic and Hindu Pallar labour, bonded to high-caste agricultural employers, is different from that of Catholic and Hindu Chakkiliyan labour bonded to Pallar employers. The struggle for the transformation of the 'idiom' of service has a different history from the history of the struggle over the use of village space. But there is a common thread in the liberating effects of adherence to a Christian church.

Not all change has been emancipating. Now that Christian missions have been abandoned and their independent patronage has vanished, Protestant Paraiyans have been forced back into servile roles.[28] Godwin Shiri, studying rural Protestant Dalits in south India, confirms that they are suffering from deteriorating debt, poverty and illiteracy, as the churches and their services disintegrate.[29]

Some Christians, particularly tribal Christians, are the object of growing communal violence, while others, particularly Syrian Christians, have seen their churches approved by the Rashtriya Swayamsevak Sangh (RSS). In the year 1999, press reports appeared regularly of the desecration of religious property, of the Sangh Parivar's accusations of 'forced conversion', of word-of-mouth hate campaigns, cases of threats, harassment and even murders of priests, nuns and missionaries.[30] The chief sites of aggression against Christians are Odisha, Gujarat, Tamil Nadu and the Christian states of the north-east. It is widely held that this persecution has no economic base. But to the extent that churches attempt to protect tribal and Dalit Christians from exploitation by Hindu moneylenders and traders, and some actively challenge oppression, religion may be the idiom of reprisal.[31]

Sikhs

The Sikh minority is not much smaller than the Christian—21 million in 2011 (1.72 per cent of the total population). Forming a large majority in Punjab, one-fifth lives in neighbouring states where Sikhs form about 7 per cent of the population, while the diaspora pervades India and reaches out to the UK, the USA and Canada. Like Christians and Muslims, despite their egalitarian religious ideals, Sikhs are segmented into sects, which are loosely associated with different sectors of the economy. Some 25 per cent of Sikhs are Scheduled Castes (of which one-third are Mazhabis), mostly poor agricultural producers and labourers with economic interests at variance with Sikh Jats. The dominant Jat landowning caste forms about half of the Sikh population.[32] With assured irrigation and with relatively large, consolidated holdings, Sikh Jats were famously at the forefront of adoption of the seed-fertilizer technology introduced in the mid-1960s. By 1981, on 1.6 per cent of India's land area, with a canal irrigation system built under colonial rule and on holdings consolidated at the time of the devastating movements of population at Partition, Punjab was producing 73 per cent of the wheat procured for public distribution by the state, and 48 per cent of all procured rice.[33] Yet, although Punjab still has the highest level of aggregate rural wealth and consumption expenditure in India, the returns to Punjab's agriculture have been notably unequal, reflecting the relatively advanced capitalist production that achieved these results.

However, 'what strikes most about Punjab is the way production and exchange are almost neatly compartmentalised on religious and caste lines. The peasants are Sikhs (Jats), merchants are Hindus (Khatris/Aroras/Baniyas). Sikhs cultivate, organise agricultural production. Hindus trade. Peasants live in villages, merchants live in towns.'[34] The religious alignment of the economy is set against a background of unbalanced sectoral development and political turbulence. While 70 per cent of rural households are Sikh, 85 per cent of urban households are Hindu. The segmentation of the Sikh *merchant* castes—they do exist, notwithstanding Singh's valid generalization quoted above—is so great that not only trade but also industry is dominated by Hindu capital. Agricultural trade is largely in the control of Baniyas whose accumulation strategy focuses on agro-industry, notably the processing of wheat, rice and oilseeds.

Trade in manufactured goods is dominated by Khatri and Arora castes. Disrupted at Partition, this trade is strongly networked into metro-capital unrelated to agriculture and outside Punjab. Despite high levels of both rural and urban consumption and its top rank in agriculture, industry in Punjab is relatively underdeveloped, ranking only tenth in industrial development. It has a distinctive structure of small-scale industry, limited to cotton processing and metalworking. This industry derives more from princely patronage prior to Partition, and to the immigration of Hindu Arora traders, than to the locally generated agricultural surplus. Even the expansion of Ramgarhia artisanal engineering is more oriented towards trade in spare parts, and repairs to agricultural machinery, than to machine production.

One explanation for this social and economic alignment attributes it to the Central state's reluctance to invest in a region bordering Pakistan. But Sikh reluctance or inability to invest in sectors dominated by Hindus is also suggested as being equally important. The hesitance or inability of Hindu trading castes to invest in productive industrial capital may play a part as well.

Whether caused by a lack of push or a lack of pull, the small-scale nature of Punjab's industry structures the demand for non-agricultural labour, which then tends to be supplied by unskilled migrants from Bihar. It repels educated Sikhs, whose unemployment rates are high. At best, they seek work elsewhere, exploiting the mercantile networks of their co-religionists abroad.

Religious Plurality and Class Formation

Religion plays a complicated role in shaping accumulation inside Punjab, even if the state's surpluses feed accumulation elsewhere in India. The structural differentiation of agriculture has been thwarted by continual, politically resented state subsidies and concessions to the Sikh religious minority, which controls a strategic national resource—foodgrains. Moreover, the communal stratification of production and trade in Punjab defines class formation. While the agricultural sector produces a commercialized surplus, exchange relations in Punjab tend to be stratified by religion. Where producers and traders compete over the distribution of the surplus, their religious alignments are accentuated. The reinforcement of exclusive religious alignments may then serve to carve a local moral space to protect and legitimize access to surplus. Arvinder Singh concludes from this that Punjab's communal conflict may be interpreted as a symptom of a transition to an industrialized, but *pluralist*, society.[35]

Jains

Jains number 4.5 million, but their economic significance is much greater than their share in the population (0.37 per cent).[36] While their epicentre is in north-west India (the desert area of Rajasthan once known as Marwar), they are distributed parsimoniously in urban and 'rurban' settlements throughout the subcontinent. With a religious philosophy of non-violence, adherence to truth and the renunciation of worldly passion, and with a claim to be caste-free and ritually egalitarian, Jains are commonly found to be relatively wealthy local merchants, moneylenders and pawnbrokers, and are divided in a complex way into two main sects, and then into further sub-sects, jatis and family lineages defined by locality and occupation. Jainism drew its first support from traders: 'it was because of their adherence to ahimsa (non-violence), that they never took to farming or agriculture and turned instead to commerce, trading and banking'[37] and to revenue collection and the keeping of village records under Mughal rulers. As James Laidlaw writes: 'The social homogeneity of the lay Jain community in subsequent millennia has sometimes been exaggerated, but the extent to which Shvetambar Jainism especially has been a religion of the commercial elite is by any standards remarkable.'[38]

The Jain mercantile diaspora developed under the Mughals and was consolidated under the British. Many of the Jain Baniya caste businessmen who laid the foundations of Indian manufacturing industry began as clerks, brokers and agents in the 'great firms' of the nineteenth century, which dealt in opium trading, banking, insurance, the wholesaling of gold, and the export of wool.

Religion, Accumulative and Reproductive Practices

The question whether Jain capital is organized in a distinctively Jain way, with implications for accumulation, has generated a rich but inconclusive body of research. It has been argued, first, that Jains are culturally distinct in business, and, second, that Jains are organized more effectively than others. On the first point, Laidlaw's insights into a Jain community working in the gem trade in Jaipur show that it is as tightly bound economically as the Tamil Muslim community described by Mines. Yet it differs from that Muslim community by being socially non-binding. 'Jain communities, because they are not closed or bonded groups, are best seen as the medium and outcome of social clustering around corporate religious property. Families tend to drift out of the community if their membership is not sustained and renewed through some combination of religious observance, economic participation, kinship and marriage links, residential proximity and day to day interaction.'[39]

As to whether Jains are organized more effectively, their marriages and alliances are a crucial basis of their capital accumulation. Jain identity structures Jain accumulation. Laidlaw quotes Richard Fox on the Tezibazaar Baniyas: there are 'business families' not 'family businesses'.[40] A family's 'credit' in business 'is its stock in the broadest sense, which includes social position, its reputation and the moral and religious as well as the business conduct of all its members . . . When a family contracts a good marriage, its credit increases . . . The potential impact on business confidence of particular potential alliances are explicit factors for consideration . . . because business practice depends . . . so much on trust, moral conduct and financial standing . . . This means that a family's credit lies not only in the hands of the men who are actually engaged in business, but in those of its women too. When sons succeed automatically to their father's position in the family firm, the future of the business enterprise is, quite literally, in the women's hands. Thus the distinctive religious division of labour in wealthy Jain families—with men making generous donations and women undertaking periodic extended fasts—has an economic dimension.'[41]

So Jain religion affects economic activity through the private sphere and its gender division of religious practice and piety.

But commercial accumulation also transcends the bounds of caste and religion. When Christine M. Cottam Ellis studied urban Baniyas in Rajasthan, half of whom are Jains and half Vaishnava Hindus, he found that Jain merchants themselves identified three areas of difference: the spatial arrangement of the business site, their accounting procedure, and the importance of public and community service. On close inspection, however, he found that in none of these respects do Jain merchants actually differ from their Vaishnava counterparts. Further, for both groups of merchants the patrilineage and its economic endeavours are synonymous. Business is a religious duty and a source of merit. Business failure is regarded by both religious groups as signifying sin or lack of religious merit. Lack of religious merit may be protected against by religious deeds. Thus, religious deeds are 'priced' in relation to assets, liabilities and commercial risks. Ellis found that credit and merit are 'cumulative, self-fulfilling and with concrete effects upon survivability, especially where competition is oligopolistic—which is the typical situation of a small market town'. She was driven to conclude that 'Jains are not culturally distinct as businessmen, nor do they form a separate economic interest group'.[42]

Parsis

In 2011, there were about 57,000 Parsis in India, about 70 per cent of whom are thought to be living in Mumbai. An equal number are believed to live abroad. Everywhere the Parsi population is declining rapidly.[43] Having farmed land in rural Gujarat for centuries, after seeking refuge there from religious persecution, Parsis migrated to Bombay some 300 years ago. There, through the conjuncture of their acceptability to the very small set of British capitalists and their experience of craft production and trade, they 'took a decisive lead in industry by establishing cotton spinning and weaving mills in the latter half of the nineteenth century and the earliest import and export firms' as well as shipbuilding and construction.[44]

There is very little literature about their role in the contemporary economy. Parsis remain important promoters in the corporate sector (where they have a reputation of being relatively progressive employers) and are prominent in the professions. However, their pre-eminence has been lost and although they are significantly wealthier and more educated than average in Bombay—a survey in

1982 showing some 40 per cent of Parsis in employment being in professional, technical and clerical posts contrasted with 22 per cent for the population as a whole—Parsi industrial capital is actually highly concentrated.[45] Parsi philanthropy, however, extending outside the religious community is an important component of collective identity, and the Parsi panchayat provides Parsis with a system of social security—for healthcare, education and the relief of acute poverty—which mitigates their inequality.

Religious Plurality and Small-Scale Accumulation in a Small South Indian Town

'The tendency of capitalism has been to do away with different manners, customs, pretty local and national contrasts and to set up in their stead the dead level of the cosmopolitan town.'[46]

The final case study is of Arni in Tamil Nadu, a place like Siliguri but half its size, an administrative centre and police station, with a complement of developmental state activity and infrastructure, retailing, agro-industrial production and trade, transport, the workshop production of silk cloth, the crafting of gold, and the finance for all this and the rural economy.[47] In Arni, we can see the religious minorities at work together in 'the dead level of the cosmopolitan town'. Together with the Scheduled Castes they constitute 35 per cent of the population, but without them, a mere 10 per cent, of which Muslims make up more than half. While Arni's Muslims comprise a great range of ranks and status, Arni's Hindu majority are for the most part relatively low caste, but the richest business families include higher caste immigrants from other regions of India. Family businesses make up 85 per cent of commercial and productive enterprises, under half of which have a wage labour force. Arni's is a distinctive form of pluralist development, one that may be as widespread in India as the 'Punjab' model in which agriculture, trade and industry are mapped on to religions. Though minorities are not scattered randomly through Arni's economy, each minority has a wide range of both niches and incomes.

While some commodities are the preserve of distinct minorities, only sanitary work (Scheduled Castes), rubbish dump scavenging (Scheduled Tribes) and recycling (Muslims) are exclusively so. Religious plurality does not lead to the suppression of competition, either between firms or in the labour market. The gender division of labour in family business cannot be disentangled from the gendered practices of religious observance. Both affect business reputations. Women in the local Hindu business elite are as secluded as their Muslim counterparts. There is no evidence that in Arni the relation between private and public spheres differs according to religions. This goes for the kinds of business family there are and the type of businesses they undertake; and this way private religious merit is linked to public economic reputation.

But differences in authority derived from religion do affect the economy. They work through the status of new occupations which can be 'genealogically' related (through the deepening of commodification) to ones which were of ritual significance in the agrarian economy. Lorry ownership, for example, requires relatively large capital, by the standards of this small town. But the status of transport, derived from bullock carting, is regarded as relatively low, so transport is mainly undertaken by Vanniar Gounders, an upwardly mobile agricultural caste. Religious authority works through the sacred qualities of things. For Hindus, rice is a purer thing than garlic and it also has no protective covering by the time it is retailed, so, although Scheduled Caste labourers may turn paddy on the drying yard with their feet, no Scheduled Caste traders handle milled rice in the main market places. Scheduled Castes do retail garlic. Unlike Hinduism, Islam declares no divine sanction against handling the recycling of waste, so, from the recycling of scrap metal from the local rice mills, Muslims have developed an increasingly complex—and now an international—

trade network for recycling plastic, card and paper, glass and a range of metals—activities they freely admit are tainted for Hindus by their association with the low Hindu caste status of scavengers and waste pickers. 'That's no concern to us,' some say, 'there is good money to be made.' Religious groups sometimes also form moral units within which distribution occurs; the Jains for instance react with solidarity and money if their co-religionists meet with accidents, sickness, alcoholism, depression and death.

In Arni, there is nothing that distinguishes those members of religious minorities who are most successful at accumulation from successful local capitalists in general. Muslims and Jains are prominent as political representatives in business associations, in philanthropical organizations (in education, housing, town development, commodity associations, the running of mosques or temples and their properties) but Hindu businessmen express their power in exactly the same ways. Differences in the way economic exchanges take place within and across religious boundaries are not marked enough for businessmen ever to have talked about them to me when I was working there. In fact, at the start of the twenty-first century, elite businessmen—both Hindu and Muslim—denied that religion made a difference to transactions. The religious groups intermix at the public rituals of marriage. There seems to be no difference due to religion in the labour process. Where the workforce is too large to be organized by kinship, the degree of 'cosmopolitanism' of their workforces cannot be explained in terms of the employer's religion.

Nevertheless, religious plurality does regulate the economy of Arni in subtle ways. Although to a lesser degree than in other parts of India, the upper-caste Hindus and Jains own most of the physical fabric of the town, and residential areas are structured by religion. This is not because religious patterns coincide with underlying segregating forces of wealth, poverty and education. Scheduled Castes and Christians do not differ materially from Jains in their access to college education, and, except for Jains and Protestants, a majority of every religious group had annual household incomes under Rs 24,000 in 1997—which was double the state's poverty line at that time. So people of all religions are quite poor, and each religion has a wide income distribution with only a tiny minority of materially secure families. Nevertheless, they do occupy urban space differently. Some Muslim businesses—cloth, sweets and hardware—are scattered through the commercial heart of town, but others, more exclusively Muslim—notably slaughterhouses and recycling—are segregated together, well within town but on the edge of the central commercial hub. Scheduled Caste people live in wards quite separate from people of other castes. Their traders face open hostility to their occupation of physical roadside space for the smallest kind of trade in fruit and vegetables. Yet they are allowed into the 'secular' territory of the state-run municipal market where they mingle with both low-caste and Muslim traders of fish and meat and with the few higher caste women abandoned by their husbands, who have been forced into trade. Through its secular control over space and place, the local state *can* be used to gain entry to economic markets which are structured to exclude Scheduled Caste people.

Religious groups sometimes form distinct units for finance. Whereas Muslim businessmen borrow from private commercial banks, Jains have banks for the exclusive use of Jains. They also have privileged access to state-regulated banks. Scheduled Castes are rarely given any kind of access to nationalized or private banks, and compensate by developing their own small but exclusive chit funds—rotating credit associations.

Religious plurality here finds much of its expression in the economy through the interventions and neglects of the state. While the state gives relatively secure employment to uneducated Scheduled Caste sanitary workers, and to some educated Scheduled Caste teachers and members of the police and armed forces, Catholics, Protestants and Muslims have to face open competition. If they benefit at all from state concessions (as one small Catholic trader did, for example, with help for start-up capital), it is the result of patronage rather than formal state policy. While political parties are increasingly aligned by caste, and their funding is increasingly based on caste and religion, the failure of local political patrons to capture state resources needed to create the infrastructure appropriate to a town of Arni's size has created a political vacuum. It is significant that this has been filled by local Muslim magnates. Muslim subscriptions and loans have backed the creation of a teachers' training college, managed by an extended kin group, registered as a trust. It suffered from a lack of legitimation, *not* on the part of local Hindu society (from which it recruits eager students from up to 40 km away) but on the part of the state. This is because the official rules of accreditation, based on standards indifferent to religion, had not been fully complied with in its initial phase.

Last but not least in this list of forms of social regulation based on religion, the 'big religion' is important for the commodity markets in which Arni's minorities must accumulate their capital. This provides the overarching ideology consistent with corporatist forms of economic regulation, the more so the smaller the relative size of the minorities. 'We live on and off the Hindus and must continue to be friends,' and 'There is no communalism here. We in Arni are secularist,' said Muslim traders in Arni, in 1994. 'Being secularist' effectively means taking the regulative institutional practices of Hinduism.

Religious Plurality and the Economy

The plurality of religions in India is clearly the result of waves of conquest, of trade, of the evolution of religions in reaction to the 'wild jungle growth'[48] of Hinduism, and finally of the particular concept of secularism adopted by the Indian state. While religious ideas deal with experiences that far transcend economic life, there is nonetheless a relationship between the plurality of religions and the economy, contrary to what mainstream economic literature might lead one to suppose. The economy would not take the form it does were it not for the social organization of religions, even though the effects are very mixed and the influence of religion varies greatly according to context.

The Triple Talaq Controversy: A Sociolegal View

Flavia Agnes

The contradictory pulls of gender, religion and politics affect the way Muslim women's rights are positioned and debated. The demand for legal reforms on the grounds of gender concerns, minority rights and identity issues has been an important plank for the Indian women's movement since the 1970s. In this context, it is important to critically analyse the recent triple talaq controversy in order to discern what it entails for the everyday life of the subaltern Muslim woman.

I wish to argue that unless the rights are located within the everyday lived realities of women's lives, they remain hollow words in a statute book. For their effective implementation, and for them to bring any significant change in the ground reality of women within these communities, these rights need to be linked to local subaltern struggles. The triple talaq controversy should not be seen as a standalone event. This is just another coordinate in the long-standing strife between community rights and gender in the communally vitiated Indian political arena. The aim of this essay is to situate the contentious issue of triple talaq in its historical context, which will reveal the constant build-up that has foregrounded the issue of the lack of rights of Muslim women under Muslim personal law in litigation during the last three decades. This will help clear some misconceptions surrounding the rights of Muslim women under the Muslim personal law regime, and will explicate why gender should not be construed as a neutral terrain, disjointed from the current political reality.

Examining the Pay-off

Amidst much media speculation, the full bench of the Supreme Court pronounced the much-awaited verdict in the *Shayara Bano* case on 22 August 2017.[1] It was not anyone's case that arbitrary and instant triple talaq is a desirable mode of dissolving a Muslim marriage. What was under contestation was the most appropriate manner for reforming the Muslim personal law: through the intervention of the courts, the legislature or through the Muslim clerics. Despite the hype created by the media in the preceding two years, which sought to give the impression that this was an open-and-shut case, on this critical issue, the verdict was split.

The operative part of the elaborate and complex ruling, comprising three different and diverse judicial opinions captured in the 400-odd pages, is just one line: 'By a majority of 3:2 the practice of "talaq-e-biddat"—triple talaq is set aside.' Though three judges pronounced triple talaq to be invalid, they differed in their reasoning for declaring it so. Justice Rohinton F. Nariman (for himself and Justice Uday U. Lalit) held that since the word 'talaq' is mentioned in the Sharia Application Act, 1937, it forms part of a statute and becomes 'law in force', and hence is amenable for being tested against fundamental rights. They thus declared it unconstitutional. The Sharia Application Act does not mention the word 'triple talaq' or 'talaq-e-biddat'. The view expressed by Islamic legal scholars is that a mere recognition of Muslim personal law by the Sharia Application Act does not give it a statutory status.

Justice Kurian Joseph concurred with this view and held that triple talaq could not be tested against the touchstone of fundamental rights. He preferred to stay within the realm of Islamic law and examined whether instant triple talaq forms an essential and core religious practice. Since the Supreme Court in *Shamim Ara* (2002)[2] had already declared instant triple talaq invalid, and had laid down the valid procedure for pronouncing talaq, he had no hesitation in concluding that triple talaq is not an essential core of Islamic law in India and hence held the same invalid. The judgment was hailed by the media and by all contesting factions as 'historic', though it merely followed the dictum of *Shamim Ara* and did not lay down any new law.[3]

Criminalizing Triple Talaq

Since the Supreme Court had declared the law on the subject,[4] initially the government issued a statement that it did not find it necessary to legislate on this issue.[5] Barely four months later, on 28 December 2017, the government, in great haste, introduced a bill in the Lok Sabha (lower house) to criminalize triple talaq on the ground that triple talaq continued unabated despite the historic ruling. There was thus an urgent need to enact a law with penal provisions as a deterrent, the government argued.[6] The contentious bill met with a great deal of resistance in the Rajya Sabha and hence could not be passed, but meanwhile the government promulgated an ordinance. Certain amendments were introduced in the bill in order to allay fears over any misuse of the law. The amendment allowed an accused to seek bail by approaching a magistrate. A provision was added to allow the magistrate to grant bail after hearing the wife.[7] After the general elections in 2019 when the National Democratic Alliance (NDA) government returned to power with even greater numbers, the bill was reintroduced. It was discussed in the Rajya Sabha on 30 July 2019. This time the Opposition unity crumbled like a pack of cards and the bill was passed with a comfortable majority. Soon thereafter, the president gave his assent to the bill that makes talaq-e-biddat (or triple talaq) a criminal offence.[8] The Muslim Women (Protection of Rights on Marriage) Act, 2019, carries provisions of a jail term of up to three years.

The ethical issue involved here is whether this Parliament—which has the least representation of Muslims—has the moral authority to enact a law without a public debate and without arriving at a consensus among the representatives of the community. The government is intending to override a well-established norm that laws for minority communities must be enacted after holding discussions with community leaders/representatives, legal experts and other stakeholders, and after striving to reach a consensus.

Several studies have shown that rather than approaching the formal structures of law, women from marginalized sections use informal community-based mechanisms to negotiate for their rights. At times women move in and out of formal and informal fora, as well as between secular and religious spaces of dispute resolution. The research of Gopika Solanki and Sylvia Vatuk provides us with valuable insights on the multiple ways in which women negotiate for their rights.[9] Anindita Chakrabarti and Suchandra Ghosh, drawing upon two years of fieldwork at a sharia court situated in a large Muslim locality in Kanpur, argue that while addressing issues arising out of family disputes, the key concerns for women are enmeshed within kinship rules, household economies and family intrigues.[10]

It is clear that against this ground reality, a law penalizing triple talaq will not help the cause of empowering Muslim women. While mere utterance of the word 'talaq' thrice may not dissolve the marriage, incarcerating the husband certainly will, as the enraged husband may resort to the approved Quranic form of pronouncing triple talaq over a three-month period, thus leaving the wife high and dry.

The government included certain clauses regarding maintenance and child custody in order to allay the concern of precarity that will surround Muslim women when the oral pronouncement of triple talaq is criminalized. These add-ons are inconsequential as there are already adequate legal provisions to safeguard the rights of Muslim women in this regard under the Domestic Violence Act (DVA) and the Muslim Women Act. It is argued that if desertion of the wife is not a criminal offence, how can triple talaq be rendered so, when the impact of these two actions upon the aggrieved woman is similar.

The more pressing concern is that the statute has the possibility of fuelling a fear psychosis within the Muslim community. This move will also strengthen the prevailing stereotypes about the Muslim community at large.

The title of the act—the Muslim Women (Protection of Rights on Marriage) Act, 2019—is meant as a throwback to the statute enacted in 1986, the Muslim Women (Protection of Rights on Divorce) Act (MWA). Despite the widespread criticism that MWA had deprived Muslim women of their right of post-divorce maintenance, this ill-conceived statute was the basis on which a sensitive lower judiciary could dispense a modicum of justice and protection to minority women. Under the statute, a divorced Muslim wife is entitled to a lump sum maintenance as fair and reasonable settlement—a right which has far more advantages for a divorced wife than the earlier provision of recurring monthly maintenance. The statute has better protected the rights of divorced Muslim women than their counterparts from other religions. Despite this, there is a deliberate attempt to portray the MWA as a statute that deprived Muslim women of their crucial right of maintenance.

The Politico-legal Quandary

How did the issue of triple talaq come before the Supreme Court in the first place? The suo motu (on its own) reference to constitute a special bench to examine discriminatory practices of Muslim law such as polygamy and triple talaq was made by a two-judge bench comprising Justices Anil R. Dave[11] and Adarsh Kumar Goel, in *Prakash v. Phulavati*[12] on 16 October 2015 while deciding an appeal concerning the rights of a Hindu woman to ancestral property. In an unprecedented manner, responding to stray comments by an advocate present in court and relying upon some articles in the press, the judges made a reference to the chief justice to constitute a special bench to examine discriminatory practices that violate the fundamental rights of Muslim women. This came to be titled as 'Re: Muslim Women's Quest for Equality'.[13]

The Constitutional Bench headed by Chief Justice Jagdish Singh Khehar heard the arguments in this matter along with four other judges—Justices Joseph, Nariman, Lalit and S. Abdul Nazeer—during the summer vacation, 11–18 May 2017. Appreciating the strategy of placing four minority-community judges on a five-judge bench, Professor Tahir Mahmood, an authority on Islamic law, commented that such a move was needed since unruly media debates had given the issue the colour of a majority-minority tussle.[14] In the same spirit, to keep a tight rein over the proceedings and to narrow down the scope of the arguments, the Constitutional Bench also declined to examine the issue of Muslim polygamy and confined the arguments strictly to whether instant triple talaq constitutes a core belief among Sunni Hanafi followers of Islam in India.[15]

Tagged along with the original reference were several subsequent writ petitions/intervener applications by individual Muslim women, Muslim women's organizations including the RSS-affiliated Rashtrawadi Muslim Mahila Sangh, the All India Muslim Personal Law Board (AIMPLB)[16] and other affiliate organizations such as the Jamiat Uelma-I-Hind, etc.

Commenting upon the manner in which this issue was used by the prime minister during his election campaign in Uttar

Pradesh, Abusaleh Shariff and Syed Khalid, relying upon the 2011 Census data, highlighted the fact that the number of deserted Hindu women who live in deplorable conditions far exceeds the number of Muslim divorcees and deserted women. The numbers are staggering: out of 2.3 million separated and abandoned women, around two million are Hindus, as against 2,80,000 Muslims. And yet no attention is paid to them, even while the prime minister was lamenting over the plight of Muslim divorcees.[17]

However, the then newly appointed chief minister of Uttar Pradesh, Yogi Adityanath (who draws his lineage from the extremist Hindu Mahasabha, and is the founder of the militant youth organization Hindu Yuva Vahini), compared triple talaq to the disrobing of Draupadi.[18] Another of his cabinet colleagues, Swami Prasad Maurya commented that Muslims resort to talaq to keep 'changing wives' to 'satisfy their lust' and leave their wives to beg on the street, which aroused the wrath of members of the All India Muslim Women's Personal Law Board who demanded his resignation.[19]

These statements from Sangh Parivar leaders illustrate the Hindu nationalist strategy of disseminating the discriminatory stereotype of the Muslim male as a sexual threat, which fuels the cultivation of masculinist heteronormativity among Hindu men. Moreover, the issues of Muslim divorce and polygamy have been projected as an appeasement to Muslim men. A petition filed by an 'aggrieved' Hindu before the Bombay High Court in 1952 ('Narasu Appa Mali') challenging the provision of monogamy for Hindus on the grounds that it discriminates against Hindus since Muslims are granted this privilege is reflective of this sentiment.[20] This judgment, in its anxiety to uphold the constitutional validity of Hindu monogamy, held that personal laws are not subject to fundamental rights. The Supreme Court has never addressed the issue of personal laws being beyond the pale of fundamental rights frontally, nor has it struck down this ruling as unconstitutional.

However, the demand to abolish polygamy among Muslims was projected as a concern for Muslim women to camouflage its communal undertone. In the recent controversy over triple talaq, the right-wing political parties projected it purely as a concern for Muslim women, though the demand was used as a stick to beat the Muslim community and to project them as backward and anti-women.

The fact that the RSS has also been campaigning for the abolition of triple talaq and had intervened in the Supreme Court reflects the tightrope walk Muslim women who are demanding a change in their personal laws are faced with when a right-wing anti-Muslim government is in power. In this situation, the ideal solution would be adopting the policy of 'reform from within', for the Muslim Personal Law Board to issue a clear statement that arbitrary and instant triple talaq is un-Quranic and hence invalid, and mandate that all divorces must essentially be through the prescribed Quranic mode of talaq-e-hasan or talaq-e-ahasan.[21] This would send a clear signal to the Muslim community. The Board's refusal to come out with such a statement led to a stalemate where the Supreme Court was compelled to intervene and declare the law.

The tightrope walk of Muslim women is also located within a context in which abstract notions of rights inherited from Euro-American liberal political traditions are present in some form in the Constitution of India under Article 14, which is premised on all being equal and having to be treated equally. However, an exception has been carved out under Article 15 (3) to provide a space for special protection to the marginalized: Scheduled Castes, Scheduled Tribes, women and children. But Muslims do not figure in this; rather, a special protection for minorities is provided under Articles 25 and 26, which is also a fundamental right. In essence, there is a tension between individual rights and group rights within the Constitution itself.

The Shayara Bano Case

BJP activist Ashwini Upadhyay had filed a petition pleading for the enactment of a Uniform Civil Code (UCC), soon after the 'Re: Muslim Women's Quest for Equality' to the chief justice was made. When the petition came up before the bench presided over by the then chief justice, T.S. Thakur, it was dismissed on the grounds that the issue falls squarely within the domain of the legislature.[22] But while doing so, the bench avowed that if a victim of triple talaq approaches the court, it would examine whether instant and arbitrary triple talaq violated the fundamental rights of a Muslim wife. So, by the time Shayara Bano received the talaqnama sent by her husband by post, the ground for filing the writ petition was firmly laid, and the mantle of being a crusader for the cause of Muslim women's rights fell upon her shoulders. It is interesting to examine the background of this case.

Initially, Bano's brother had contacted a Supreme Court lawyer to transfer the case filed by her husband in the family court at Allahabad, for the restitution of conjugal rights (in effect, to ask her to return to the matrimonial home—a far cry from 'instant triple talaq'), to her native place in Kashipur in Uttarakhand.[23] Since Bano did not want to return to her husband and instead wanted to contest the case after it was transferred to Kashipur, to bring to an end the long-drawn litigation the husband's lawyer resorted to the frequently used device and sent a talaqnama by post to Bano.

When the talaqnama was brought to the notice of her lawyer in the Supreme Court, he advised his client to file a public interest litigation (PIL) on the grounds that the talaqnama violated her dignity, though Shayara Bano has consistently maintained that she does not wish to return to her abusive husband. While the case brought a great deal of publicity, Bano's core concerns— access to her children, regular monthly maintenance, and a fair and reasonable settlement for the future; issues which had to be litigated in the local magistrate's court, under relevant statutes, the DVA and the MWA—remained unaddressed.

It was rather tragic that during the entire period while the triple talaq controversy was raging, the media continued to project that Muslim women are devoid of rights rather than dwell upon the entire judicial discourse which had held instant and arbitrary triple talaq invalid. The conspiracy of silence regarding landmark rulings such as *Danial Latifi* in 2001[24] (which upheld the right of a divorced Muslim woman to a lump sum amount as fair and reasonable settlement for the future) and *Shamim Ara* has caused Muslim women great injustice.

The Conspiracy of Silence

In 2002, in the landmark *Shamim Ara* ruling, the Supreme Court invalidated arbitrary triple talaq and held that a mere plea of talaq in reply to the proceedings filed by the wife for maintenance cannot be treated as a pronouncement of talaq, and the liability of the husband to pay maintenance to his wife does not come to an end through such communication. In order for a divorce to be valid, talaq has to be pronounced as per the Quranic injunction.

In the same year, a full bench in the Bombay High Court in *Dagdu Chotu Pathan v. Rahimbi*[25] had held that a Muslim husband cannot repudiate the marriage at will. The court relied upon the Quranic stipulation: 'To divorce the wife without reason, only to harm her or to avenge her for resisting the husband's unlawful demands and to divorce her in violation of the procedure prescribed by the Shariat is haram.' All stages stipulated in the Quran— conveying the reasons for divorce, appointment of arbitrators, and conciliation proceedings between the parties—are required to be proved when the wife disputes the fact of talaq before a competent court. A mere statement in writing or oral deposition before the court about a talaq given in the past is not sufficient to prove the fact of a valid talaq.

These judgments in turn relied upon two earlier judgments of Justice Baharul Islam pronounced in 1981 while presiding over the Gauhati High Court. In the first case, *Sri Jiauddin Ahmed v. Anwara Begum*,[26] the court had held that though the Muslim marriage is a civil contract, a high degree of sanctity is attached to it. While the law recognized the necessity of dissolution of marriage, it could be effected only under exceptional circumstances and for a reasonable cause. An attempt at reconciliation by two relatives—one from each of the parties—is an essential condition precedent to talaq.

Later in the same year, a division bench of the Gauhati High Court presided over by Justice Islam in *Rukia Khatun v. Abdul Khalique Laskar*[27] affirmed the earlier legal position as follows:

The correct law of talaq as ordained by the Holy Quran is:

(i) Talaq must be for a reasonable cause; and (ii) it must be preceded by an attempt at reconciliation between the husband and wife by two arbiters, one chosen by the wife from her family and the other by the husband from his. If their attempts fail, talaq may be effected.

Following *Shamim Ara*, there were a plethora of verdicts that declared instant triple talaq invalid and safeguarded the rights of women approaching the courts for maintenance.[28] The settled position in law can be summarized as below:

i.   Talaq must be for a reasonable cause.

ii. Talaq should be pronounced only after reconciliation attempts have failed. Appointment of an arbitrator, one from each side to help in the reconciliation as stipulated in Verse 4:35 of the Quran, is mandatory.

iii. Talaq may then be pronounced once (even if three talaqs are pronounced at one time they are to be treated as a single utterance).

iv. Talaq must be followed by a waiting period (iddat) of three months. For pregnant women, iddat is until the conclusion of pregnancy.

v.   Talaq can be revoked mutually at any time during the iddat period and the parties can start living together.

vi.   If differences cannot be resolved during the iddat period, the husband must fulfil all his contractual obligations towards his wife—return of mehr (payment made by groom to the bride at the time of marriage), valuables, belongings, payment of maintenance for the iddat period and a full and final settlement for her and her children for the rest of their life (as per the provisions of the MWA, 1986).

If the husband and wife resolve their differences after the iddat period, a fresh marriage contract, with a fresh mehr, would have to be entered into before resuming their marital life.

Despite this, the mainstream media continued to project a biased view that once the husband pronounces talaq, the wife is stripped of all her rights. This bolstered the misconception that a husband who pronounces instant triple talaq is absolved of his legal obligation of providing maintenance to the wife. Ironically, even women's rights groups working with Muslim women to empower them became co-conspirators in this conspiracy of silence as they too endorsed the view projected by the media that Muslim women are bereft of rights. So they did not help Muslim women to approach the court to enforce their rights in local courts which the superior courts had secured for them.

It is due to the selective amnesia regarding the struggles of Muslim women over several decades and the heightened Islamophobia prevailing within a majoritarian Hindu nationalism[29] that the hype around the issue of triple talaq was created and sustained. Within this political scenario, the petition filed on behalf of Shayara Bano came to be hailed as the first instance where a helpless Muslim woman, who is devoid of rights, had challenged the validity of triple talaq.

I am reminded of Zakia Pathak and Rajeswari Sunder Rajan's famous essay, 'Shahbano'. To justify the perverse formulation that 'Hindu men are saving Muslim women from Muslim men', the Muslim woman must invariably be projected as devoid of rights and lacking agency, and the Muslim male as conservative, lustful, polygamous and barbaric.[30]

The intent behind these legal reforms in postcolonial India is more anti-Muslim than pro-women. A careful analysis of events in the postcolonial Indian legal history provides clear evidence for the same. While the MWA, 1986, was widely criticized for being anti-women, the amendment of 1976 to the Special Marriage Act (SMA), 1954, passed unnoticed. The 1976 amendment was the first instance in the postcolonial history of India when the move towards UCC was reversed. By the amendment, if two Hindus married under the Special Marriage Act then the secular code which granted equal rights to men and women, the Indian Succession Act of 1925, would not apply to them, and the parties would continue to be governed by the Hindu Succession Act which ensured male coparcenary rights. The amendment was both anti-women and anti-minority. It sought to protect the property interests of a Hindu male who married any woman within the broad Hindu fold by not depriving him of his coparcenary right. At the other level, it served as a deterrent to a Hindu male wishing to marry a woman from the minority religious communities because then he could be penalized by forfeiture of his rights to ancestral property.[31]

As a lawyer defending women's rights, it is not my argument that Muslim women must continue to suffer gender unjust practices until broader community concerns are resolved. But the current political reality demands a more nuanced and pragmatic approach to address these injustices. I contend that personal laws for different communities are gender discriminatory in their own unique ways. Small and significant reforms within personal laws have more relevance for the welfare of women of different communities. The above assertion has also been upheld by the 21st Law Commission which has recommended reforms in respective personal laws to achieve the broader goal of gender equality.[32]

The Violence of Law

Manisha Sethi

As I started to write, Sadhvi Pragya declared a two-day vow of silence as penitence for calling Gandhi's killer a true 'patriot'. Her outburst—swiftly condemned by her party officially—was triggered by the film-star-turned-politician Kamal Haasan's denunciation of Nathuram Godse as the first 'Hindu terrorist'. Nevertheless, the BJP did field Pragya Sadhvi in the 2019 general elections. A key accused in the Malegaon blasts of 2008—it was the motorcycle registered in her name on which the bombs were mounted—Pragya was said to have been an important cog in the Hindutva terror network of Abhinav Bharat.[1] This network allegedly conspired and executed multiple blasts through 2007–08, the most significant among them being Samjhauta Express, Mecca Masjid, Ajmer Sharif and Malegaon.[2]

In 2014, when the BJP swept to power, the cases against Pragya and other accused tottered—amidst revelations by the special public prosecutor that the National Investigation Agency (NIA) had asked her to go slow—with acquittals in one case after another.[3] These acquittals have provided grist to the Hindutva apologia mill that the NIA, a specialized agency set up by the United Progressive Alliance (UPA) in the aftermath of the Mumbai carnage in

November 2008, had spawned the bogey of Hindutva terror at the behest of the Congress Party.[4] Pragya was granted bail on medical grounds under the Maharashtra Control of Organised Crime Act (MCOCA). While some charges have been dropped, she has not been discharged, nor acquitted in the Malegaon blast case, which still proceeds apace. The BJP president though declared that Pragya had been fielded as a 'satyagraha', surely a moral form of protest, against those who had coined the abomination 'saffron terror'. Recall that in 2013, the then home minister, Sushilkumar Shinde, citing intelligence reports, had used the term in the aftermath of a series of arrests, from Pragya to Lt Col. Prasad Purohit to Swami Aseemanand.[5]

Pragya's candidature and indeed her electoral victory would avenge this patent injustice and validate the BJP–RSS charge that Hindus cannot be terrorists.[6] Even in 2013—which seems strangely distant from the politics of the present moment—this was hardly a minority view. Our popular culture, films, news media had assiduously built the narrative of Islamic terrorism. Custodians of law subscribed to it with ardent conviction. M.N. Singh, a former police commissioner of Mumbai and who had led the investigations into the 'Black Friday' blasts of 1993, condemned 'saffron terror' as a 'politically coined terminology . . . very handy for some people to counter the charge of jihadi terrorism'. 'In my opinion,' he concluded, 'there is nothing like saffron terrorism. It just doesn't exist in the Hindu pantheon [sic].'[7] The Sanatan Sanstha and Abhinav Bharat, according to him, were localized phenomena, which had been 'nipped in the bud' by the NIA. Terrorists of the Hindu variety—oxymoronic as they are, even if they exist—lack the capacity, the capability, the resources, but above all 'even the motivation'. Of course, Singh did not rule out the possibility of involvement of some Hindu groups, but their actions were to be classed as 'retaliatory attacks as opposed to organized homegrown terror sponsored by Pakistan'.[8]

How could Hindus possibly bomb their own country—except in retaliation? The idea of Hindus as the only true and natural citizens of India has long been elevated to the mythical. As is the binary between a violent Islam and a non-violent Hinduism.

But what of the law itself? Surely, law is inert, or blind, and the rule of law is the bedrock of any democracy. Surely, the law does not discriminate, caring little for reigning bigotries. Even a cursory study of the working and history of anti-terror laws is likely to disabuse one of this naiveté to reveal that in fact the law serves to further embed these prejudices—offering itself as a very useful tool to criminalize sections of society.

Enacted in 1985 following the assassination of Indira Gandhi and originally promulgated for areas designated as 'terrorist affected'—essentially Punjab—TADA quickly spread out, and at the time of its expiry a decade later, covered twenty-three states and two union territories. It departed dramatically from the principle of procedural fairness by allowing for the admission of confessions made before police officers, added new offences of abetment of terrorism without precisely defining 'abet', introduced summary trials and truncated appellate procedures, and permitted secret witnesses, which severely affected the accused's right to cross-examine and defend themselves.

I would argue that, whether the motive or not, TADA has been used to quell dissent, suppress movements and torment minorities. And all of this results from a law legislated by Parliament, and which the Supreme Court, despite a notable challenge, declined to strike down. In Punjab, thousands of people, virtually all of them Sikh, were arrested under TADA, but statistics also show that by August 1994, Gujarat had arrested 19,263 people under TADA—even more than in Punjab![9] In 1994, the National Commission for Minorities (NCM) documented that 409 out of the 432 arrested under TADA in Rajasthan belonged to minority groups.[10] Once when activists belonging to the right-wing Vishwa Hindu Parishad were arrested under the Act, L.K. Advani fulminated against it in Parliament and the charges were dropped.[11]

Between the 1970s and 1990s, when struggles over land and labour intensified in Bihar, and bitter armed conflicts between the landless (almost always Dalit) and landlords (almost without fail upper caste) broke out, the violence of the landless Dalits was met with the most draconian law at the disposal of the state: TADA.[12] Even in the few instances when TADA was applied to leaders and foot soldiers of the upper-caste private militias, it was swiftly withdrawn.[13] It came to an end finally in 1995, when Parliament allowed it to lapse when it was due to be reviewed and extended. The large-scale outcry that this law was a mechanism of persecution also received substantiation from Justice Ranganath Mishra, the then chairperson of the NHRC. Mishra, in a letter to parliamentarians in early 1995, appealed to them to not renew the law, dubbing it 'draconian in effect and character' and 'incompatible with our cultural traditions, legal history and treaty obligations'.[14]

The might of POTA, which was enacted in March 2002 in an extraordinary joint session of Parliament, too felt disproportionately on minorities, besides political dissidents. In Gujarat in 2002, while the Prevention of Terrorism Ordinance (POTO) had not even been formalized into an act, the state government filed charges under POTO against sixty-two Muslims (including seven minors) for their alleged involvement in the Godhra train burning. Though public outcry forced the government to withdraw the charges then, a year later, POTA charges were reintroduced in the case against 121 individuals.[15] In contrast, no one was ever charged under the anti-terror law for the mass violence and brutality against the minorities that occurred thereafter. Moreover, nine omnibus conspiracy cases were filed under POTA against Muslims for planning terrorist attacks in retaliation for the communal violence.[16] By 2004 in the state, more than 280 individuals had been charged under POTA, all but one of whom were Muslim.[17] In Andhra

Pradesh and Jharkhand, studies found POTA being used as a tool of political vendetta and suppression.[18]

Despite evidentiary shortcuts, the rate of conviction for TADA and POTA could never rise over 3 per cent, leading many to conclude that the purpose of this law was not to secure convictions, but only to arrest, detain and charge people—and ultimately to keep groups (sometimes socio-religious, at other times political collectives) within the pale of criminality.

UAPA Fortified

As evidence of its malfeasance piled up, the UPA repealed POTA when it assumed office in 2004, but in a sleight of hand, bled many of its harshest provisions—barring the admission of custodial confession as evidence—into the pre-existing Unlawful Activities Prevention Act. A chapter on terrorism was added, and through subsequent amendments in 2008 and 2012 it has been further made to resemble the dreaded POTA. There is then the story of how a fortified UAPA has extended all that was wrong with POTA and earlier TADA, erasing in one stroke the history of resistance against these laws. Here though I want to cast my focus on how the seemingly benign sections of UAPA that came into existence in 1967 have unintentionally or otherwise proven vital in consolidating and naturalizing the connections between Islam and terrorism.

Section 3 of UAPA empowers the government to proscribe an organization if it came to form an opinion that its activities and objectives were secessionist, it promoted enmity between different groups of people, or was prejudicial to national integration. While earlier the ban was to be valid for two years, requiring the executive to furnish new grounds for imposing a fresh ban at the end of those two years, the law was amended in 2012 to extend the period of the ban to five years. So first, this law provides the government sweeping powers to curb peoples' right to association for prolonged periods, and second, this power can be mobilized on the basis of the ideological and subjective understanding of what constitutes national interest and what comprises anti-national or secessionist activity and objectives.

Section 10 of the law lays out the penalty for continuing to 'be a member of an association declared unlawful by a notification issued under Section 3'; Section 13 delineates the punishment for assisting in 'any unlawful activity of any association declared unlawful under Section 3'. We may add here that the amended UAPA in 2008 brought into being Section 20 which states that 'any person who is a member of a terrorist gang or a terrorist organization, which is involved in terrorist act, shall be punishable with imprisonment for a term which may extend to imprisonment for life, and shall also be liable to fine'. As the Bombay High Court noted in 2013, this is very equivocally worded, and if interpreted narrowly, it could be in conflict with Article 19 of the Indian Constitution.[19]

UAPA thus provides an iron legal framework for pronouncing guilt by association, and the law itself lends to be used for purpose beyond its statement of objects, and is liable to be misused. It is indeed the state's position in the course of trials that under the provisions of UAPA, 'the mere association with the members of the said Organization and the mere possession of the literature/material propagating the philosophy or ideology of the said organization amounted to an offence'.[20] Hence, people can be arrested on the basis of merely an accusation that they are members of a banned outfit even if they have not participated in any violence. These are not merely procedural infirmities. The courts' occasional warnings that prosecution and agencies must differentiate between active and passive membership, and mere membership and sympathy cannot be grounds for criminalization[21] are only feeble safeguards against how these cases are prosecuted and tried.

Moreover, one must remember here too that the definition of unlawful activity as 'an act or by words, either spoken or written, or by signs or by visible representation or otherwise' itself is so wide as to render possibly any human activity as suspect. My concern, therefore, is that anything that the government does not approve of could have the potential of being consigned to the overflowing category of unlawful. Granting bail to the members of the cultural troupe Kabir Kala Manch, the Bombay High Court observed that none of the accused had been alleged to have resorted to violence, or alleged to have handled weapons or explosives, or alleged to have committed a terrorist act. The nature of allegations and the bulk of evidence against the accused was that they sang songs and performed theatre wherein they raised the issues of caste violence, farmers' suicides and social inequalities, which were shown to reflect 'communist thought'. As the Bhima Koregaon case—which continues to unfold dramatically since 2018, bringing within the circle of suspicion an increasing number of activists and academics—amply demonstrates, legitimate political activity is easily demonized and illegitimated through this law.[22]

In September 2001, just days after the horrific 9/11 in the USA, the central government banned the Students Islamic Movement of India (SIMI) for the first time through a gazette notification. Interestingly, though the government claimed that SIMI glorified Osama bin Laden and Masood Azhar, and even had links with Al Qaeda, the government's own records showed that up until 1999, no cases of violence had been registered against members of the organization. Indeed, the only crimes they were charged with were cases of making speeches, or pasting and distributing posters, which challenged the dominant ideas of Indian nationalism. It was only after the BJP came to power in 1999 that charges of violence began to be levelled against them.[23] It may be noted here of course that none of the organizations indicted for spreading hatred and even caste and communal violence by a long list of inquiry commissions—be it the Madon Commission on the Bhiwandi riots of 1970 or the Srikrishna Commission investigating the Bombay violence of

1992 have been deemed unlawful. So what violence is worthy of proscription and which may be tolerated or ignored reflects the biases of the executive.

The declaration of SIMI as unlawful was followed by a spate of arrests with raids at various SIMI offices. But as we shall now show in the remainder of this section, over the long period of time since 2001—during which the ban has been renewed and reimposed in 2003, 2006, 2008, 2010, 2012, 2014—the ban has become an easy handle for the police and investigative agencies to randomly pick, detain and then arrest and frame Muslim youth, ostensibly on charges of carrying on the activities of the banned organization.

Sections 3, 10 and 13 of UAPA, 1967, have been invoked against scores, if not hundreds, of Muslim youth across the country. Some of these men had been active in SIMI prior to its ban; some had outgrown the organization because they had crossed thirty years—the age limit for membership in the organization—some were guilty of having acquaintances, friends or relatives who had been involved or had been office-bearers in SIMI; and some fell conveniently in the demographic that could be passed off as SIMI.

How does the law work? The twin arteries of UAPA are firstly, membership (of unlawful organizations) and secondly, conspiracy (of furthering the activities of the unlawful organization). Both, membership to an organization that no longer exists legally, and nebulous charges of furthering the activities of such an organization, are notoriously difficult to pin down, especially in the absence of any alleged violence. Often, the only 'proof' that the investigating agency is able to demonstrate to connect the accused to a proscribed organization and their participation in unlawful acts is through confiscation of banned and seditious literature from the custody of the accused. In a study of Madhya Pradesh, it was found that out of seventy-nine UAPA cases registered against Muslim youth between 2001 and 2010, only one consisted of an allegation of violence—and that too a shoot-out in the Teen Pulia area of

Khandwa district in November 2009, in which three people, including an Anti-Terrorism Squad (ATS) constable, died.[24]

Reading the first information reports (FIRs) filed in the early days of the ban in 2001, one may assume that former members and office-bearers of the organization were overcome with a sudden death wish. While their officers were being raided and sealed, and police and agencies were conducting a 'crackdown' nationwide, SIMI activists and sympathizers allegedly appeared in public places, shouting slogans, waving pamphlets, pasting posters, exhorting others to join the newly banned organization, vowing to resist the ban on SIMI, and provoking a Muslim insurrection against the government. And invariably, they were all apprehended in the middle of their unlawful activities and a rich haul of material seized from them. Never mind that these recoveries consisted of issues of SIMI's erstwhile mouthpiece, *Islamic Movement*, copies of which surely would be in the possession of SIMI members on the evening of the declaration of the ban, and which were perfectly legal to possess; posters inviting people to conferences long past when the association was wholly lawful; or simply literature in Urdu or Arabic—somehow always deemed a sign of unlawfulness. Even Ghalib's couplet *'Mauj-e khuun sar se guzar hii kyun na jaae/Aastaan-e yaar se uth jaaen kyaa'*[25] was seen as an intimation of some dark terrorist conspiracy and seized as incriminating material by the police in Solapur.[26]

With time, it appears that supplies of 'SIMI literature' started to wane, and in later cases we began to see photocopies of *Islamic Movement*, SIMI receipts and other magazines making their appearance. FIR no. 184/2008 PS Khajrana, for example, tried to pass off photocopies of the cover and back pages of an old copy of *Islamic Movement* as pamphlets! Magazines such as *Tehreek-e-Millat*, registered with the Registrar of Newspapers for India (RNI), and never declared banned, and even a newspaper cutting of *Dainik Jagran*, which carried a news item about the narco-analysis test of Safdar Nagori, an ex-office-bearer of SIMI, have been pounced upon as evidence of continuation of the activities of an unlawful association. Identical copies of *Tehreek-e-Millat* with the name 'Rafia' written on its cover by hand appears in the evidence list as *Tehreek-e-Millat Rafia* in two cases from Madhya Pradesh, and four cases of Maharashtra, including in the Malegaon 2006 blast case. The last, one should remember, was laid at the door of SIMI, and among the proof was this magazine. In 2013, the NIA filed a fresh charge sheet against Abhinav Bharat operatives, and the original so-called SIMI accused were finally discharged by the NIA court in 2016.[27]

For another illustration, in which UAPA is deployed to frame Muslims, let us turn to the Kota case of 2008. Three months after the serial blasts in Jaipur in 2008, the Muslim neighbourhood of Kota allegedly saw a spate of police raids. Several men were picked up. They were only wanted for routine *pooch taach* (questioning) in connection with the blasts, no charges were to be pressed, the police repeatedly assured the frightened men and their families. Days of alleged illegal detention and torture later, these men were accused of spreading communal venom against Hindu gods and goddesses, speaking against national unity, integrity and secularism, of involving Muslim youth in anti-national activities, and of carrying on activities for SIMI despite it being outlawed. All of these charges remained vague, with neither the FIR nor the charge sheet making any precise link to any specific terror activity. Nonetheless, elliptical allusions to the Jaipur and Ahmedabad serial blasts were made by the police, and the newspapers didn't take long to present them as key suspects in these blasts.

Four and a half years later, the court acquitted the accused. Of the forty-three witnesses lined up by the prosecution, thirty-eight turned hostile, swearing in court that they had been made to sign blank papers by the police. The so-called proscribed literature seized by the police turned out to be perfectly legal, as it dated to before the ban. And finally, the prosecution had failed to secure the sanction of the central government, as is required when certain sections of UAPA are invoked.

Media trials, which link the accused to acts of terror they are not even formally charged with, are conducted, and bail applications rejected repeatedly by lower courts. The prosecution hopes until the last moment that no one will notice the missing sanction.

According to recent National Crime Records Bureau data, two-thirds of UAPA cases end in acquittal,[28] which is rather low when compared to the average rate of conviction for non–terror-related crimes, which stands at 45.1 per cent. The flimsiness of evidence and the sketchiness of charges has resulted in scores of acquittals, as in the Kota case, but equally true is the fact that the overwhelming nature of the 'war on terror' discourse has allowed the conviction of many even in the face of glaring lack of evidence. Over the years, therefore, we can notice a disturbing trend of capitulating to the hype of terrorism to mete out convictions even in the absence of evidence. To give just one example, in one of the most prominent SIMI cases from Madhya Pradesh, known commonly as the Pithampur case (FIR no. 120/2008), the court conceded that though nothing documentary had been placed before it by the prosecution to prove the accused's culpability in any unlawful activity, 'this does not have an adverse impact [for the prosecution's case] because it is not usually possible to find such proof; one cannot in fact expect or desire formal proof'.[29] The court convicted the accused.

The Limits of Reasonableness

UAPA presents itself to be a reasonable law since it provides an opportunity to the proscribed group to argue its innocence and appeal against the unjustness of its ban in a tribunal headed by a sitting judge of the high court. In *Jamaat-E-Islami Hind v. Union of India*,[30] where UAPA was challenged as unconstitutional, the apex court, though upholding its constitutionality, had warned that the tribunal is not required to provide 'merely its stamp of approval' to the opinion already formed by the Central Government. It was expected to 'itself assess the credibility of conflicting material on any point in controversy and evolve a process by which it can decide whether to accept the version of the Central Government or to reject it in the light of the other view asserted by the association.'[31] In reality though, the reasonableness is only a chimera. The only organization which has contested the ban consistently since it was banned is SIMI, and every time, but for 2008, the tribunal upheld the ban on the basis of secret documents provided by the state in sealed envelopes, to which representatives of SIMI had no access.[32] For example, the tribunal, in upholding the government ban on SIMI in 2010, noted that the director of the Ministry of Home Affairs had produced material related to SIMI in sealed covers. Further, having examined these secret files of the central government, the presiding judge concluded, 'I am satisfied that there was due and adequate application of mind before the order under Section 3(1) of the Act was made on whether or not ban on SIMI should be reimposed.'[33] The lawyers challenging the ban, it must be noted, could only cross-examine the home ministry's official on that what was submitted in official records, not on what was contained in the sealed envelopes.

In denying the proscribed group any real possibility of defence, the law inverts established principles of jurisprudence and principles of natural justice. Indeed, the very fact of former office-bearers contesting the ban in the tribunal was described by the state as 'proof' of the banned organization's continued activities! In 2008, when Justice Gita Mittal, heading the tribunal, revoked the ban citing the scarcity of evidence and facts that could lawfully sustain it—as opposed to the plenitude of allegations—the central government rushed to the Supreme Court, securing a stay on the tribunal pronouncement the same day.[34]

It is impossible to divorce the registration of this large number of cases from the unabated ban on SIMI. On the one hand, these cases validate the extension of the ban; before every tribunal, home departments of various states provide a list of FIRs and cases in which alleged SIMI operatives have been booked. Though theoretically these cases should pertain to the period since the expiry of the previous ban, that is, these cases must be fresh, it is not unknown for the home departments to pad up their files with cases booked much earlier too. And of course the home departments do not draw attention to the acquittals in the cases they had presented before the previous tribunals, which would risk exposure to accusations of malicious prosecution. We might also remember here that the tribunal is only quasi judicial in nature, thus allowing for submission of self-incriminating disclosures and confessions which have no value in a criminal trial. In effect, what happens is this: cases are booked, presented before the tribunal as certain proof of the continuing unlawful activities of SIMI, of which a vast majority are subsequently unable to withstand the standard of proof in a criminal trial, but in the meantime this material becomes the basis for outlawing an association.

On the other hand, the ban legitimizes the witch-hunt in the name of combating the 'terrorist organization'. It becomes a pretext for booking cases. In the aforementioned Pithampur case, thirteen leading 'SIMI activists' were arrested on 27 March 2008, following which the senior superintendent of police (SSP), Dhar, shot off letters to SSPs of various districts of Madhya Pradesh asking for the registration of similar cases. These letters immediately set off a chain reaction, resulting in eighteen cases within one month, and another four over the next six months. This surely must have been a record of sorts! How can we be sure that it was the SSP's letters that produced this result? Not only do some of these cases so registered make an explicit reference to this letter (for example, FIR no. 180/2008, PS Neemach Cantt, 8 April 2008), the investigating officer of the case, B.P.S. Parihar, himself produced eighteen of these letters in the SIMI UAPA tribunal in 2010.[35]

The ban is extended citing the large number of 'SIMI' cases, and Muslim youth are arrested and charged for being members of SIMI on flimsy grounds. It is a tragic tautology that has played out for the past decade and more. Over time, the law becomes an alibi for criminalizing an entire community. And when eight undertrials accused of being SIMI members are killed on-camera after a dramatic but suspicious jailbreak in Bhopal, their alleged affiliations can be mobilized to justify the killings. Indeed, the killings can be termed a 'morale booster' as a central minister did,[36] and the then chief minister can ask innocently if the terrorists should be fed 'biryani'[37]—a cultural trope if there was ever one.

Entrenching a Regime of Suspicion

Exceptional laws such as TADA and POTA that diverged from the constitutional rights framework, taking the plea of national security and integrity, used to come with the inbuilt sunset clause of periodic legislative review. Parliament would determine, from time to time, whether the situation still demanded the operation of such an exceptional law or not. So, in 1995, ten years after it came into being, TADA was not renewed by Parliament. POTA was repealed in 2004 after mounting evidence of its lawlessness. UAPA, however, despite the provisions drawn from exceptional laws— even in its original avatar—pretends to be a part of an ordinary legal regime and lacks a sunset clause.

When UAPA was amended in the immediate aftermath of the Mumbai carnage in November 2008, it was given more teeth, including extended periods of detention, allowing prosecution greater leverage to file delayed charge sheets, designating an increasing circle of acts as 'terrorist'. L.K. Advani, the BJP's leader in the Opposition, lamented that it still lacked POTA's power, namely allowing confessions made before police officers admissible as evidence.[38] The Gujarat government had tried repeatedly, unsuccessfully, to promulgate the Gujarat Control of Organized Crime Act (GUJCOCA) on the lines of the dreaded MCOCA, in order to have at its disposal a law that could short circuit constitutional principles and protections afforded to all citizens against the brute might of the state. Passed originally in the Gujarat Assembly in 2003, GUJCOCA provided for custodial confessions and intercepted telephone conversations as admissible evidence, and was returned thrice between its passage and 2009. In 2015, it was renamed the Gujarat Control of Terrorism and Organised Crime Act and passed again by the state assembly, receiving finally presidential assent in November 2019.[39] One might dismiss as election bombast former home minister Rajnath Singh's speech during the course of an election rally at Mirzapur in Uttar Pradesh that upon their return to power in 2019, the new government would enact a sedition law so stringent that it would send shivers down the spine of 'anti-nationals',[40] but it is of a piece with the party's idea of a muscular state, its implicit disdain for civil liberties and individual freedoms. Certainly, the most recent amendments to UAPA passed in the very first parliamentary session after the new government took office herald an even harsher punitive regime of suspicion. In August 2019, Parliament agreed to grant the government powers to designate individuals as terrorists under a fourth schedule—even before any charges have been brought against them, and before any judicial process has indicted them of wrongdoing.[41]

Relentless arrests and their reportage—especially of those belonging to a particular community—bolster the perception of the nation being under siege, of dark conspiracies being afoot, thus justifying the application of extraordinary laws, legitimizing the robbing of our rights. Indeed, they move us to acquiesce to the erosion of our own rights for the larger good of the nation. But they also further culture wars, by filling the threatening figure with ethnic markers and telling us—sometimes subtly, but mostly rather crudely—as to who constitutes the authentic national, and who endangers that pure nation.

And so, Sadhvi Pragya takes oath as a member of Parliament—the NIA insisting now that her motorcycle on which bombs were mounted is 'insufficient evidence'[42]—while scores of those acquitted after years of being accused as 'SIMI' operatives struggle to put the pieces of their broken lives together.

The Crisis of Citizenship and the 'Bangladeshi' Paradox

Tanweer Fazal

In the Constituent Assembly, as the chairman of the Constitution Drafting Committee, Dr B.R. Ambedkar rose to present Articles 5 and 6—containing provisions defining Indian citizenship—his exasperation was more than obvious. He reminded the members that within the Drafting Committee, this was a subject that gave the greatest 'headache', and ultimately what was being presented was only a draft which satisfied 'most people, if not all'.[1] The two articles attracted an unprecedented number of petitions for revisions—'a veritable jungle of amendments' in the words of Dr Rajendra Prasad, the president of the Assembly.[2] The imprints of Independence, scarred by the ferocity and intensity of Partition violence, were evident in the deliberations of nationalist leaders as they set out to define the contours of membership and entitlements of former subjects who were to achieve the status of rights-bearing citizens.

A huge inflow of 'refugees' from areas now constituting Pakistan required a special provision for their legal membership. But then there were also a good number of those who had briefly migrated to Pakistan before returning to their homeland. These were seen as men (and women) of divided loyalties, whereas citizenship demanded unflinching allegiance. The clamour in the house was to have a citizenship law that either denied or restricted their acquisition of Indian citizenship. Irrespective of the secular and composite character of Indian nationhood, members also wished to replicate an Israel brand of law of return for the Hindu and Sikh citizens of other Asian and European countries. In this case, their loyalty was presumably given, and members pursuing this line of argument demanded no further test.

The members of the Constituent Assembly absorbed themselves in the problems thrown at them by the turn of history. In essence, the question that confronted all of them was: what kind of a republic did India visualize itself to be? Citizenship was at the centre of the Indian vision, prompting questions such as: would nationality or cultural markers have a bearing on citizenship? Or would it privilege a section of the citizenry over the 'other' defined in terms of beliefs, origins and mother tongues? Apart from the range of entitlements that citizens could enjoy, the problem of citizenship showed up in terms of developing a sound principle that was sufficiently inclusive as much as exclusive, assigning a date of arrival or departure to the shifting populations, determining the status of kinsmen living outside India as much of those born to non-citizen parents.

Unmoved by the majoritarian cries that resonated in the Assembly, the Indian resolution of the vexed problem was remarkably non-partisan, much in line with the secular foundations of the national movement. Prime Minister Jawaharlal Nehru was categorical in this regard: 'All these rules naturally apply to Hindus, Muslims and Sikhs or Christians or anybody else. You cannot have rules for Hindus, for Muslims or for Christians only. It is absurd on the face of it.'[3]

Attentive to the multiplicity of cultures and persuasions, jus soli (right of soil) found favour over triumphalist calls to make ties of religion, ethnicity or nationality—jus sanguinis (right of blood)—the basis of citizenship. The Indian Citizenship Act, 1955, conferred citizenship on the basis of birth (to everyone born between 1950 and 1987, and thereafter to anyone born to Indian citizens), descent (born to Indian citizens outside India), naturalization (foreigners who have lived in India for twelve years or more) and registration (valid immigrants with a continuous stay of seven years).

Idea of Belongingness and Authenticity

Over the years, however, a new surge in ideas of belongingness centred around religious and linguistic exclusivity, son-of-the-soil movements, tribalism and ethnicity have come to severely interrogate and, to an extent, impair this vision of universal citizenship. Migration flows across various regions, much a reflection of lopsided development, complicating the problem further. Bihari labour is welcomed in labour-starved areas of Punjab and Haryana, but bereft of its citizenship entitlements. The politics vents its pent-up aggression on Hindi speakers. North-easterners in Delhi and elsewhere are constantly reminded of their alienness, and 'outsiders' often invite physical violence for transgressing the sacred lands of the north-eastern tribes. Prejudicial classifications of Indians and non-Indians, Indics and non-Indics, citizens and non-citizens, national homes and ethnic homelands have returned to haunt the culture-blind foundations of Indian citizenship.

Assam today, home to a diverse range of communities and cultures, is in the throes of a crisis of citizenship. Histories and partially preserved memories of migration, violence and marginality are recounted to define the alien and the native, the loyal and the suspect, the Assamese and the so-called East Pakistanis or Bangladeshis. Most often, it was the Bangla-speaking Muslim who attracted the greatest ire. Early echoes of this crisis of faith in secular citizenship could be heard in the Constituent Assembly too:

I have been told by . . . some honorable members of this House
that after Partition as many as three times the Hindu refugees
from East Bengal, Muslims have migrated to Assam . . . with a
view to make a Muslim majority in that province for election
purposes . . . those who come from sinister motives, from
motives of occupying lands and usurping the rightful owners
by terrorizing them and becoming a majority in this country,
it is up to us to say that no asylum would be offered here. . . .
Their object is only to create trouble here.[4]

Bangladeshis as 'Termites'

In the forerun to the 2019 Lok Sabha elections, Home Minister
Amit Shah (then president of the BJP) termed the 'Bangladeshis' as
termites and swore to disenfranchise and weed them out. Not only
were they a threat to national security, they ate up the resources
meant for the poor, he maintained.[5] It could be deduced that the
epithet 'Bangladeshi'/'infiltrator' was reserved only for the Muslim
immigrants (the Miyas), as Shah assured the Hindu, Sikh and
Buddhists amongst them of guaranteed citizenship.

The backdrop of Shah's aggressive postures is two extraordinary
official measures that though initially peculiar to Assam hold
the potential to foment miseries all round. The Supreme Court
monitored the updating of the National Register of Citizens,
an exercise to detect undocumented migrants, those who had
supposedly arrived after the cut-off date of 24 March 1971. The
Citizenship (Amendment) Bill, 2016, on the other hand, serves as a
bulwark for immigrants of Hindu, Jain or Sikh persuasions against
the consequences of the NRC. In tandem, both the NRC and
the proposed amendments end up stigmatizing and vilifying the
Muslim Bengali (the Miya) in Assam.

The draft register, issued in 2018, left out some four million—
nearly one tenth of the population of the state—putting their
citizenship status under a cloud of doubt. The final NRC,

published a year later, eventually managed to exclude nearly two million people. The process of updating the NRC required that the residents prove their ancestry with a 'legacy ancestor' whose presence was recorded either in the NRC of 1951 or other 'legacy documents' prior to 25 March 1971. The resolutions offered to mitigate this existential crisis range from expulsion, to rendering them second-class status—stripped off their political rights, left with work permits at the most. The process of producing immigrants and foreigners out of citizens has involved partial reading of the history of migration, fabricating categories, ignoring statistics, the suppression of truth, and silences around targeted violence.

Production of the Foreigner

Intriguingly, the foreigner, nay Bangladeshi, defiled and demonized as s/he is, had a rather delayed appearance in the Assamese psyche. It certainly did not coincide with the formation of the new state of Bangladesh in 1971. Early attempts to mobilize Assamese nativism were centred on an adversary far more generic—the *Bohiragoto* or the outsiders, which included a range of communities: the Marwaris, the Nepalis, the Adivasis and the Biharis, as also the Bangla-speaking Hindu and Muslim immigrants. It was precisely this imprecision in converging on a single adversary that the Anti-Bohiragoto movement, despite the support from the middle classes and the regional press, failed to cut much ice amongst the ordinary Assamese. The shift in emphasis towards the 'Bangladeshi' found immediate reverberation in the Assamese-dominated Brahmaputra valley of Assam. Typically, the 'Bangladeshi' was a Muslim, a small or marginal farmer or a wage-worker in the fields, who took up the least remunerative but most arduous work in the towns and cities, and lived precariously in the *chars* (islands) of the Brahmaputra. Not only did it have definite ethnic attributes, it corresponded with the 'Miyas', whose discomforting presence in the state was no less than a century old.

In the late 1970s, Assam's political theatre reverberated with a massive mobilization of students, professionals and other sections of the urban middle class, with calls to throw out the foreigners residing in the state. The upper-caste-dominated Assamese press voiced the awakening of Assamese subnationalism.[6] The native intellectuals provided a narrative of victimhood—a rationale for the Assamese angst. The chief reason behind the outburst against the foreigners, it was argued, was long years of colonial exploitation of the state's resources by both foreign and Indian capital. Taking a leaf out of Lenin's conceptualization of nationality movements, left intellectuals overlooked chauvinist tendencies, and equated it with the upsurges of 'oppressed and backward nationalities'. In this broad polarity of the exploiter and the exploited, the foreign capital, the 'Indian' big bourgeoisie, the non-Assamese petty traders and shopkeepers as well as the migrant peasantry came to be presented as the oppressor. On the other hand, the native bourgeoisie, the middle classes as much as the Assamese peasantry and labour were assumed to betray no relationship of exploitation among them. Assam's ethnic other—the undefined outsider—oppressed them all.

Histories of immigration were rewritten and Assam was presented as reeling under tidal waves of 'influx' of immigrants supposed to have encroached upon 'indigenous' lands and invaded native culture. It was a narrative of blood and prejudicial ideas of belongingness that citizenship was expected to adhere to. New constructs of 'indigene', 'immigrant', as also 'infiltrator' emerged as key social categories to refer to specific communities of people living in the state. Broadly speaking, the Asamiya ethnic community, and the tribes claimed indigeneity, irrespective of their own histories of arrival. The term immigrant is reserved for the Bengali speakers, regardless of their antiquity of presence. The term infiltrator, borrowed from Hindutva constructs, specifically refers to the undocumented Bengalis, mainly Muslims, who supposedly entered the state from Bangladesh after 24 March 1971.[7]

Immigration, a Contested History

In 1998, the then governor of Assam and retired army general, S.K. Sinha, submitted his report on 'illegal immigration' to the government of India. The report is significant as it is often cited as the official recognition of the impending crisis. Sinha categorically separated the case of the 'Hindu refugees' from that of the 'Muslim infiltrators'. While the immigration of the former had ceased by 1971, it was the latter's continuous 'influx' which, for Sinha, had disturbed the demographic balance. Its plausible outcome was the Assamese being reduced to a minority in their own land. This, for him, was evident from the population figures, where Muslims, during 1971–91, had returned much higher growth figures. Palpably, a few of Assam's districts were Muslim-majority, and this, for Sinha, posed a challenge to national security and its resources. It was only a matter of time 'when a demand for their merger with Bangladesh may be made', he cautioned.[8]

A decade and a half later, a division bench of the Supreme Court, in its order mandating a time-bound process of the NRC update for Assam, made a similar observation. While admitting that any estimate of immigrant population was difficult to ascertain, the Court joined the chauvinist chorus of an unabated infiltration by immigrants from neighbouring Bangladesh. It held on to the view that the immigrants were largely Muslims who could be susceptible to 'ideological support' from Islamic fundamentalists envisioning 'a larger country comprising Bangladesh and the entire North-east'. In an observation that could have far-reaching implications, the Court discovered a 'direct correlation between the rise of fundamentalism and increase in influx' of foreigners.[9]

In the absence of any exact count of undocumented immigrants residing in the state, various spurious speculations and rough approximations are routinely floated. Most often, the figures are contradictory, complicating the problem further. The All Assam Students' Union (AASU)-led Assam movement thrived on inflated figures of immigration and 'Bangladeshi influx'. Bisweswar Hazarika, a supporter of the movement, put the figure at as high as 77 lakh, nearly 50 per cent of the state's population then. AASU, in one of its publications, placed the number of 'infiltrators' at more than 45 lakh, of which at least 15 lakh, it speculated, had managed to enter the electoral rolls. After signing the Assam Accord, in which 1971 was accepted as the cut-off year, the movement leadership put the figure of foreigners so defined at 20 lakh.[10] Efforts at scientific estimation too failed to yield any consensus owing to the conflation of categories such as immigrants, refugees and infiltrators, paucity of data, and historicity of the problem.

The tendency of the Muslim population to return a relatively higher growth rate frequently triggers alarm bells, and is often cited as incontrovertible evidence of a 'continuous influx' of Bangladeshis into Assam. For example, on the publication of Census 1991 data on religion, which showed a 4 per cent rise in the Muslim population of Assam, *Asam Bani*, an Asamiya weekly, attributed the excess growth rate of the Muslim population to the large-scale immigration of undocumented Bangladeshis.[11] However, the demographics are interesting, and far more complex than what is portrayed. From the census figures, it is evident that since 1971, instead of an explosion in population allegedly owing to the inflow of Bangladeshi immigrants, Assam has been experiencing a steady decline. Compared to the previous decade when the state's population grew at 34 per cent, the regression in the decade 1971–81 was sharp, a fall of more than 10 percentage points, which helped the state to restrict its growth figures to less than the national average. In fact, all through the four decennial periods, the state's population has grown (barring 1981–91) at a notch or two lower than the all-India rate of population increase. The period 1971–81 oddly coincides with the high tide of the Assamese movement centred around the bogey of the foreigner/ Bangladeshi. This definitely busts the Assamese self-belief of being inundated by a relentless stream of immigration, nay infiltration, since March 1971.[12]

Similarly, while, on the face of it, a relatively higher growth rate of the Muslim population in Assam, compared to the state's Hindu population and the all-India Muslim growth rate, bolsters the case of Bangladeshi influx, a nuanced view finds little merit in it. Economist Vani K. Barooah compared Muslim and non-Muslim growth rates of Assam's population with their respective national averages since the early years to estimate the excess Muslim or Hindu population in the state. The figures so obtained were then adjusted with the outflow of non-Muslim and Muslim populations from the state. The net presence of migrants in the period 1971–2011, according to the estimates, was 'virtually zero'. Thus, 7,30,000 persons entered Assam in the tumultuous years of 1971–91, of which 5,02,000 were Muslims and 2,28,000 non-Muslims. But an estimated 4,52,000 comprising 2,09,000 Muslims and 2,43,000 non-Muslims migrated out of the state in the period 1991–2001. This trend continued in the next decade too, as 2,83,000 people consisting of 1,68,000 Muslims and 1,15,000 non-Muslims left the state. Going by this estimate, there is no alarming rise in the number of foreigners in Assam. In Barooah's estimate, the migration figures actually show a net outflow of 5000 people between the years 1971–2011.[13]

Multiple Legalities and 'Doubtful' Citizens

Nearly fifty years since the cut-off date (24 March 1971) and more than three decades since the signing of the Assam Accord (1985), the final draft of the NRC was published on 30 July 2018. The final draft ended up excluding nearly 40 lakh residents (one-tenth of the population of the state) from being counted as rights-bearing citizens. For the leaders of the Assam movement, the exercise was a vindication of their long-nurtured conviction that the state had been deluged with the unrestrained arrival of Bangladeshis.

Questions have been raised over the process too, which smacked of inherent prejudices. Of the fourteen documents that could be produced for proof of citizenship, two—the 1951 NRC and 1971 electoral rolls—were declared to be legacy documents, and through a string of other documents, the residents were required to prove their kinship with the legacy ancestors, those whose name appeared in the two legacy documents.[14] Though the NRC intends to target the post-1971 immigrants into Assam, at root the mammoth exercise emerges from a 'crisis of citizenship' linked to the more-than-a-century-old Bengali immigration into the territories of Assam. Rather than resolving this crisis, the NRC process actually opened up old wounds and fault lines in the social fabric. In the course of registering genuine citizens, the NRC officials split the state's residents into 'original inhabitants' and the rest. For the 'original inhabitants'—a euphemism for those bearing Assamese or tribal surnames—a mere certification from the panchayat samiti was passable. More stringent tests were in store for those not deemed to be original residents. For them, even a valid family tree could run them into trouble if other claimants to the same legacy contradicted it.

The introduction of the Citizenship (Amendment) Bill, 2016, lacked even this fig leaf. It promised to grant citizenship to non-Muslim immigrants from South Asian countries on the grounds that they were victims of religious persecution, denying the same to Muslim immigrants. Cut from the same cloth as the dominant Hindutva constructions, the bill was an official validation of a cynical distinction between encroachers and refuge-seekers, between infiltrators and immigrants, between Muslim and non-Muslim settlers. In a nutshell, the NRC and the Citizenship (Amendment) Bill were products of two different majoritarianisms—Assamese and Hindutva—that appeared to be at loggerheads with each other. For the Bengali Hindu, if the NRC was a nightmare, a question mark on her citizenship, the Citizenship Bill could be a saviour. For the Muslim Bengali, however, both the NRC and the Citizenship Bill offered no respite from unremitting stigmatization, and the spectre of disenfranchisement and denationalization.

The insatiable hunt for the archetypal Bangladeshi—more a cultural artefact than a legal entity—took recourse in regimes of exception, resulting in far greater ignominies than an ordinary Indian resident would have had to bear in the course of affirming her citizenship. As early as 1950, the state government adopted the Immigrants (Expulsion from Assam) Act, 1950, which empowered it to declare the presence of any person or group to be inimical to the interest of the state, and thus order their expulsion. In the decades following Independence, it aided the local police in persecuting Bengali Muslims on the pretext that they were illegal Pakistani nationals. In 1962, an even more stringent Prevention of Infiltration of Pakistani Nationals into India (PIP scheme) Act was promulgated, which allowed the Assam government to expel nearly 6 lakh Bengali Muslims within a period of eight years (1962–69).[15] This was followed by the state of Assam deciding to set up tribunals in accordance with the Foreigners (Tribunals) Order, 1964, which promised a fair investigation by the border police, including giving an opportunity to the suspected individuals to prove their citizenship.[16]

In 1983, in response to the demands of the anti-foreigner movement, the central government promulgated the Illegal Migrants (Determination by Tribunal) Act (IMDT), which aimed at identifying and expelling illegal migrants who had crossed international borders on or after 25 March 1971. The act authorized the central government to set up tribunals that could take up what came to be known as 'applications' and 'reference' cases. Officials and residents of the state could file applications against suspected foreigners. Apprehending the plausible misuse of the provision, the act also provided for certain 'checks and balances'. Thus, only a person living in close vicinity could make an allegation, with supporting evidence and witnesses. In the case of references (persons identified as foreigners as per the Foreigners

Act, 1946), the act gave the individual thirty days to furnish evidence in his/her favour. The built-in safeguards in the act came to be viewed by Assamese nationalists as designed to facilitate rather than to frustrate migration. Demands to repeal the IMDT Act reverberated primarily among the Assamese section of the state's population. For the supporters of the act, the safeguards provided pre-emptive defenses against wanton labelling and harassment. Eventually, in a decision that seemed to have yielded to the anti-foreigner campaign, the Supreme Court struck down the act as unconstitutional.

State practices rely on a multiplicity of legal instruments and methods to signify someone as 'Bangladeshi', mark them, rip off their civic and political entitlements, incarcerate and eventually exterminate them. Since the last two decades (1997 onwards), the Election Commission began earmarking D-voters or doubtful voters whose enfranchisement is terminated forthwith. An estimated 1,25,000 Bangla-speaking Muslims, some Hindu Bengalis and Koch Rajbongshis populate the category of D-voters in the state. More noteworthy is the implicit casualness and arbitrariness of the process of their identification and stigmatization. Once marked as a doubtful voter, the only recourse are the foreigners' tribunals, and on being spurned by the tribunals, individuals are left to languish in poorly provisioned detention centres. Apart from the D-voters, incarcerated in the detention centres are also a large number of those clubbed as 'reference cases'. The 'border police' wing of the Assam police is entrusted with the task of routinely identifying and deporting foreign nationals. The suspect cases are referred to the foreigners' tribunals, where the case is dispensed with either as acquittal or in the form of virtually unending imprisonment in the detention centres. The anomalies in the process of identifying foreigners is highlighted by the fact that only a fraction of the people suspected as foreigners and referred to the tribunals were unable to produce documents certifying the authenticity of their citizenship. Amongst those stamped Bangladeshi (or foreigner) by the tribunals, the majority were ex-parte judgments suggesting grave shortfalls in the process.[17]

Evidently, the crisis of citizenship in the state of Assam is grave. It calls into question the historiography and demography of immigration, forging of ethnic and territorial boundaries, and construction of analytical and cultural categories such as authentic, indigenous, immigrant, refugee and infiltrator. The inevitable convergence of Hindutva majoritarianism and Assamese chauvinism, although seemingly at odds with each other, produces the Bengali Muslim or the Miya as an ethnic outsider, the 'foreigner', until proven otherwise through a tedious bureaucratic process. The whole exercise throws open far too many questions than it could answer. The constitutional vision of an unencumbered citizen, with no ethnic qualifications, upholding the principle of jus soli as against jus sanguinis, is today under stress. The NRC and, to a greater extent, the proposed citizenship amendment are an affirmation of the latter. With nearly 1.9 million residents declared non-citizens, what is in store could be far worse than what has been witnessed so far. Cries for adopting the NRC and establishing detention centres in the entire country are petrifyingly audible, and sooner than later bear the potential to acquire a xenophobic character.

Kashmiri Pandits: The Ambiguous Minority

Ankur Datta

What makes a 'minority'? Is it primarily a matter of population and numbers? Is a minority made by claims to land or territory? Are minorities defined by being placed outside a dominant moral and territorial order? How do numbers intersect with the question of socio-economic and political difference and power? These questions become especially important when we consider the Hindus of Kashmir, better known as the Kashmiri Pandits. With origins in the Kashmir Valley in Jammu and Kashmir, the Pandits are Hindus from a territory where a majority of the population in numerical terms is Muslim. If we consider numbers by themselves, the Pandits are indeed a minority. However, they are a minority shaped by their spatial and political location in a region marked by dispute, violence, conflict and displacement since the end of colonialism in South Asia.

In this essay, I will explore the situation of the Pandits as a minority. The essay first situates their location in the context of the history of Jammu and Kashmir from the colonial period to the contemporary, which is largely defined by a conflict involving a movement demanding the independence of Kashmir from India and the Indian state which seeks to violently supress that movement. The essay then discusses briefly the past of the Pandits and situates their location in the social and economic history of the Kashmir Valley until their displacement from their homes in Kashmir during 1989–90 with the outbreak of conflict. Following this, I discuss relations between Pandits and Muslims and Kashmir and conclude with a discussion of lives after displacement.

Situating Jammu and Kashmir

Jammu and Kashmir as a territory and region is a patchwork state, put together with the end of the final Anglo–Sikh War in 1846 and the consolidation of British colonial domination in northern and north-western South Asia. Jammu was ruled by Dogra chieftains who were vassals of the Sikh kingdom of Punjab. Gulab Singh, who was the chieftain of Jammu at the time of the final Anglo–Sikh War, had remained neutral and did not come to the defence of Punjab. His neutrality was rewarded by the British by being recognized as the maharaja of Jammu and Kashmir, which consisted of Jammu; Ladakh, which he had conquered earlier; and the vale of Kashmir which was sold to the Dogras for Rs 75 lakh. The British allowed Gulab Singh to form a princely state that was affiliated to the British empire, but which also permitted the establishment of a buffer zone between British India and Russian imperial expansion in Central Asia.[1]

The period of Dogra rule in Jammu and Kashmir embodies many of the contradictions of the colonial experience. Lasting a century, colonialism in Jammu and Kashmir saw the establishment of the modern state and bureaucracy which enabled the governing of populations on one hand and the extraction of resources and taxation on the other hand. This period was also marked by regional differences between Jammu, Kashmir and Ladakh as well as the privileging of Hindus at the expense of Muslims, even though in actual numbers, the majority of the subjects of the kingdom was Muslim.[2]

The history of the Kashmir Valley has seen periods of rule by outsiders before the arrival of British colonialism in South Asia. At different times, since the sixteenth century, the valley fell under the rule of the Mughals, followed by Afghan and Sikh domination, which ended with the establishment of colonial and Dogra rule. For many Kashmiris, decolonization has not necessarily restored them from the governance of outsiders. From 1931, a movement had begun in the valley organized by Kashmiris to demand *azaadi* or independence from Dogra rule. This movement, while connecting with anti-colonial struggles in British India, did not necessarily become a part of the Indian nationalist movement.[3] At the time of Independence and the birth of the new nation states of India and Pakistan, the status of the princely states came into question. One solution lay with Jammu and Kashmir becoming a part of Pakistan owing to the majority of its subjects being Muslim. Yet the conventional narrative also situates India's claim on Jammu and Kashmir as it would be a Muslim majority state in contrast to the other constituent states in India and hence reinforce its claim to be a secular state.[4] While these narratives need further interrogation elsewhere, they also indicate the effect of framing populations in terms of religious majorities and minorities as seen elsewhere in South Asia too and especially in the events leading to the partition of India.

The presence of armed conflict in the region begins first with the question of accession: whether Jammu and Kashmir would accede to India or Pakistan, though a third option—an independent state—was never considered by the Indian nor the Pakistani nation state. While Hari Singh, the last maharaja of Jammu and Kashmir, was yet to decide, the dominant narrative is that an invasion had taken place from Pakistan on the kingdom, forcing Hari Singh to look to the Indian state for assistance. Eventually the Indian Army moved into Jammu and Kashmir with the maharaja accepting accession to India. Thus, by 1948 began the first war between India and Pakistan over Jammu and Kashmir. This narrative misses out the fact that in 1946 a rebellion against the maharaja had begun in Poonch in the mountainous region between the plains of Jammu and the Kashmir Valley.[5] This narrative also misses out the effect of the partition of India with the arrival of refugees from west Pakistan into Jammu and the killings of many Muslims in Jammu, though the valley saw no form of communal violence.[6]

Jammu and Kashmir ostensibly had a special relationship with India through Article 370 which permitted a separate constitution and greater autonomy, though this article has been recently abrogated.[7] In any case, this relationship was marked by a degree of manipulation where Kashmiri politicians critical of India were often removed. Politicians who worked with the Indian state in turn focused on building their own power and networks of patronage which enabled a great deal of corruption.[8] This 'denial of democracy'[9] also gave the impression that the Indian state supported corruption and disregarded Kashmiri aspirations. This state of affairs continued from 1948 until the 1980s. In 1987, a coalition of political workers calling themselves the Muslim United Front contested elections and appeared to have the mandate of the people.

This resulted in discontent leading to the outbreak of conflict in the form of different militant groups which had received support from Pakistan. The militant groups varied from Islamist groups to ostensibly more secular groups such as the Jammu Kashmir Liberation Front. However, the Indian state responded with a disproportionately violent programme of counter-insurgency and militarization of the landscape. Apart from militant groups, the movement for independence includes organizations that do not practise militancy, and follow non-violent forms of political work. These organizations work under the umbrella organization known as the All Party Hurriyat Conference, which consists of different parties that demand azaadi, follow peaceful means of protest and advocacy, and refuse to participate in what they call mainstream politics and thereby boycott elections.

What affects any discussion is the fact that this is an ongoing conflict pitting Kashmiri nationalism against the Indian state which regards Jammu and Kashmir as an inalienable part of India, regardless of the sentiments and history of the Valley. What perhaps complicates any discussion is the presence of religion, where the majority of its inhabitants are Muslim. The movement is often presented in India as a fundamentalist movement supported by Pakistan. While some militant groups are sympathetic to Islamist ideologies, can the entire question of independence be reduced to a form of religious extremism?

In turn, within India, there is a framing of Kashmir not only as an inalienable part of the Indian nation state but also as integral to its Hindu nationalist ideas whereby only the pre-Islamic period of Kashmir's history is recognized.[10] While the Kashmir Valley is indeed important for the history of Hinduism as the site of numerous pilgrimages and as the birthplace of the northern school of Shaivism, it becomes a 'territory of desire' within a Hindu nationalist imagination.[11] In the process, the conflict becomes sadly caught in the mode of a 'clash of civilizations', between so-called Muslim Kashmir and the Indian Republic, which is also caught in a contradiction between its secular republican credentials and its Hindu nationalist form which has come to dominate the contemporary.

What about the Kashmiri Pandits?

Accounting at one time for a small minority in the Kashmir Valley, the Kashmiri Pandits were an integral part of life in Kashmir and were spread all across the valley until the outbreak of conflict.[12] Following a series of targeted attacks and a larger climate of fear, the vast majority of them had fled their homes in Kashmir to places south, such as Jammu. Most Pandits are now to be found outside Kashmir, either in Jammu or in cities like New Delhi. Their departure is either blamed on militants who targeted them owing to their religion and alleged allegiance to the Indian state, or on the machinations of the Indian state and the governor of Jammu and Kashmir, Jagmohan, as a means of discrediting the movement for azaadi.[13] As a result, the displacement of the Pandits has become controversial. Since the early 1990s to the present, it remains a point of contention and has affected relations between the Pandits and the Muslims of Kashmir. Their displacement also seemingly places Pandits and Muslims on the opposite sides of a line, akin to the framing of Hindus and Muslims in India, Pakistan and Bangladesh. Given this context, what does it mean to be a Kashmiri Pandit? Where do we locate them now politically and socio-economically?

The term Kashmiri Pandit itself is relatively recent as an honorific granted to Kashmiri Brahmins who worked for the Mughal court. Otherwise the Hindus of Kashmir were known then as Bhattas, a term which is used even now among Kashmiris, both Hindu and Muslim. All Kashmiri Hindus are Saraswat Brahmins, divided between two sub-castes: Gors (priests) and Karkuns (those involved in secular professions).[14] It is common to hear Kashmiris, including Muslims, speak of the Pandits as the 'original inhabitants' of the Valley. It is not uncommon to hear Muslims speak of themselves as people who used to be Pandits, thereby suggesting a conflation of being Hindu with being Pandit or a Bhatta.

As Kashmiris, the Brahmins have remained the only Hindu caste in Kashmir with the arrival of Islam in the Valley in the fourteenth century. What is interesting is that the Kashmiri Pandits themselves had developed a corpus of modern texts in the twentieth century which drew from understandings of modern ethnology and history writing. Authors such as Anand Koul, Jia Lal Kilam and R.K. Parmu all wrote and composed histories which located the origins of the Valley in the mythic poem *Nilamata Purana*. What is particularly intriguing is that their histories move through different periods of rule by Hindu kings followed by the arrival of Islam which in turn follows a particular treatment.

The advent of Islam in the fourteenth century is treated as the beginning of hardships for the Bhattas who faced persecution by the establishment of a sultanate. Conditions became so difficult that many Pandits had left the Valley to survive. When I conducted research among Pandits displaced since 1990, I would often hear people refer to these past displacements. The figure of Sultan Sikander, described as 'Butshikan' or iconoclast, holds a special place as it was in his reign that persecution of the Pandits became extreme, prompting Pandits to leave. It is in the reign of Sikander's successor, Zain-ul-Abidin, that their fortunes changed. When Zain-ul-Abidin fell very ill, he was saved through the efforts of a Brahmin physician. As a reward he ended the persecution of the Bhattas and invited them to return to Kashmir. Due to their acquisition of education they gained a significant position in Kashmir by working for state bureaucracies.

The histories I refer to continue to follow different periods from the Kashmiri Sultanate to Mughal, Afghan and Sikh domination. The Mughal and Afghan periods are treated as particularly difficult times when Kashmiris, and especially Hindus, were persecuted. This persecution ended with Sikh and Dogra rule following the establishment of colonial rule and the kingdom of Jammu and Kashmir. This contrasts with other approaches to Kashmiri history which focus on the periods of Mughal, Afghan, Sikh and Dogra rule as times of hardship due to persecution by outsiders, and for some Kashmiris, the governance of Kashmir as a part of India is an extension of that history. Published Pandit histories, however, emphasize mainly their experiences and framing as victims.[15]

Having said that, victimhood is not the only frame at hand. Kilam's history, which features chapters of prominent Pandits over the years, also portrays them as a people who achieved success. One of the features of any discussion of the popular history of the Pandits is that they are upper-caste Brahmins who valued education and acquired a high level of skill. This enabled them to obtain employment in various levels of the bureaucracy in different regimes. Their access to the bureaucracy contributed to an image of being seen as people with a relatively high socio-economic status, connected to power and influence over the large mass of the Muslims of Kashmir. While a narrative of migration as a means of survival has a mythic quality which also acquires greater force with their current state of displacement, historians such as Kusum Pant[16] and Henny Sender[17] have documented how in the eighteenth and nineteenth centuries, many Pandits had migrated to different parts of north India. Acquiring proficiency in languages such as Farsi and later Urdu and English, which became the languages of governance and business during British colonial rule, the Pandits were well placed to obtain positions of influence in precolonial and colonial bureaucracies and gradually other white-collar professions. This also gave rise to the emergence of prominent diaspora in cities such as Delhi and Lucknow. As I was often reminded by respondents from my research, the Kashmiri Pandits had given India the Nehru family, who were Kashmiri Pandits settled in northern India.

Many Pandits remained in Kashmir working for different governments in the colonial and postcolonial periods in all kinds of positions and were also prominent landowners. Older Pandits who had seen life in the first half of the twentieth century would point out that much of the student body at modern Western-style schools established in Kashmir and influenced by visiting Europeans was largely Hindu. Nevertheless, many Pandits also led ordinary lives working in low-level positions of the bureaucracy, ran small shops and businesses, or were small landowners, and who perhaps would share more with working-class Muslims, if not with agricultural labourers. Still, the Pandits became associated with a sense of eliteness. This continues to have ramifications on understanding their relations with Muslims, which shall be explored in the next section.

Kashmiriness: Pandit and Muslim Relations

One of the themes in the study of Kashmiri society and culture that is critical to this discussion is with regard to the relations between the Pandits and Muslims. Communal relations in Kashmir have been complicated by the conflict and the departure of the Pandits in 1990. In that sense, their displacement serves as a critical event,[18] recasting how Kashmiris regard the past and approach future possibilities. How are relations between Pandits and Muslims hence to be understood, critically and with nuance? What are the contours of this relationship that allow for complexity without flattening that relationship into something absolute?

One place to begin this discussion pertains to the ideology of Kashmiriyat, which refers to an identity that draws on region and language and hence allows for acknowledging religious diversity. It is an ideology that receives a great deal of patronage by political parties as well as the Indian state for overcoming difference. Yet there have been critiques of this ideology which do not necessarily argue for religious difference. One critique offered by the anthropologist T.N. Madan[19] argues that in practice Kashmiris did not overtly articulate this ideology. Based on research in rural Kashmir in the 1950s, Madan argues that while language and territory are common to Pandits and Muslims who lived side by side, everyday interactions were marked by processes of mutual cooperation and avoidance. However, Muslims provided important services such as labour, food supplies, and even served as attendants at Hindu cremation grounds. What emerges here is that for the Pandits, rules of ritual purity influenced interactions. While in different parts of India, certain services such as funeral attendants were provided by other groups in the Hindu caste system, these services otherwise provided by Hindus of lower caste status were provided in Kashmir by Muslims. What is interesting is that Madan also points out that Hindus remained dependent on Muslims for everyday needs, though Muslims need not have that sense of dependence. What also emerges is the framing of relations between Pandits and Muslims on the grounds of caste and socio-economic status.

The ideology of Kashmiriyat has been critiqued on other grounds as well. As historians such as Chitralekha Zutshi[20] have shown, ways of belonging to Kashmir have been dynamic, changing and adjusting to the demands of different forms of politics in the precolonial, colonial and postcolonial periods. Kashmiriyat is an apolitical ideology that does not account for aspirations and their complexity and contradictions on the questions of belonging and community. This becomes essential if we approach modes of belonging in relation to both shared spaces and the accommodation of differences in relation to power. Take, for instance, Madan's discussion of mutual avoidance and cooperation, where in a way the language of caste plays a role in shaping relations between Pandits and Muslims to some extent. Yet the problem of status is also further complicated by other markers of socio-economic difference such as class. As discussed in the previous section and in further detail elsewhere,[21] the Pandits were seen as elites, either as white-collar workers, intermediaries with the state or as landlords and employers of Muslims.

This sense of difference on the basis of status seems to circulate among Kashmiris—Muslim and Pandit. When I conducted fieldwork in Jammu, many Muslims would speak of Pandits as elites who would oppress Muslims they hired as labourers. Many Pandits I met would speak of themselves as being 'rajas' or kings. Such claims of socio-economic difference and hierarchy easily connected to political processes, especially as many Pandits worked at different levels in the state. Political differences could also take other forms and experiences. In a memoir written about life in the period between 1947 and 1990, Sudha Koul, a Pandit woman, describes her feelings when Jawaharlal Nehru visited the valley. For Koul and others, this was a matter of pride as Nehru, India's first prime minister, was a Kashmiri Pandit. She writes about being shocked then on coming across a small protest against Nehru.[22] Her account did not demonstrate anger or fear. Rather it suggested an incomprehension of a different political aspiration and sentiment, which nevertheless was growing. It also suggests a tension that appears when a mass movement of any kind in Kashmir on any issue has to contend with a public that is also mostly Muslim. Where then do we locate Kashmir's Hindus?

There were indeed some Pandits who saw things differently, such as the political activist Pandit Prem Nath Bazaz who did not see Kashmir as a part of India.[23] The question of differences based on faith affiliation did indeed matter politically, though it needs to be explored in a nuanced manner to avoid fixing the Hindu and the Muslim in Kashmir in a state of permanent opposition, but rather as identities being worked upon. This can be seen in different situations and examples, such as the first organization working for independence during the colonial rule known as the 'Muslim Conference' which became the National Conference to be more inclusive, the use of religious sites as spaces of mobilization (as seen elsewhere in South Asia), to the work of activists such as the Kashmiri Pandit Kashyap Bandhu who sought to reform Pandits in small ways such as asking Pandit women to wear sarees, a garment apparently more 'appropriate' for Hindus. The discussion of religion as a component of political life has been a complex process for all Kashmiris historically, especially in trying to work out how to be a Muslim or a Hindu.

Conventional reporting on Kashmir, from the perspective of the Indian state, often ignores Kashmir's complex social history and focuses on what is considered a clear form of Islamist politics. While communal relations in Kashmir and differences require further study, they must also be handled with care as they also flatten the picture. Many Kashmiri Pandits were indeed elites, due to their levels of educational attainment and their professional status. The land reforms of 1953 in Jammu and Kashmir, where surplus land was redistributed to the tillers, were significant as many Pandits were badly affected, which indicates their levels of landholding.[24] Studies of Brahmin populations in different parts of India, such as south and western India, share a similar history with the Pandits, who were landlords and critically served as bureaucrats in the colonial administration, which enabled them to acquire a great deal of influence. In the process, as the upper castes, their work enabled them to also become a part of the middle class within a modern political economy.[25] Similarly, to imagine the Kashmiri Pandits would imply imagining them as a middle-class population.

Yet they comprised a range of the middle class, from influential bureaucrats, lawyers, justices, writers, doctors, teachers and so on and all the way down to serving as low-level clerks and peons, jobs that neither paid well nor were of particularly high status. Hence, there was a great deal of differentiation among the Pandits themselves. As a respondent of mine would often point out, *khandani* Pandits, or those who came from old, established families, would only interact with other khandani people, whether they were Pandit or not. The image of the elite does not apply as a blanket form and there were and remain many Pandits who were not wealthy, not highly educated, who lacked influence and faced economic hardship. The image of the Pandit elite falls flat among the Pandits who had spent two decades in camp colonies for displaced persons in Jammu and now lead dead-end lives in low-income colonies such as Jagti, built by the state for displaced Pandits who have no property elsewhere.

While points of difference between Muslims and Hindus may seem distinct, there are also many stories of friendship, intimacy and other bonds that speak to mutual care and support between Pandits and Muslims. Alongside stories of anger, rage and criticism among Kashmiris, I would also come across memories of exchanging gifts on festivals such as Shiv Ratri and Eid or very simply of picnics with friends, especially among the older generation of Kashmiris. While these forms of connections are too ordinary for politics, they matter immensely.

After Displacement

The mass displacement of the Pandits from Kashmir that took place during 1989–90 represents one of the most drastic cases of internal displacement in South Asia. What is striking about their flight is that within a few months, the vast majority of the Pandits had fled the Valley to seek sanctuary in places to the south such as Jammu, with small groups relocating to Kathua, Udhampur and even the Delhi National Capital Region. The exit south was not an organized affair and many families I had met during the course of my research reported leaving on their own without telling anyone—not even friends and neighbours.[26] For instance, one man I met in a camp in Kathua had revealed that they left when they realized other Pandits had left without informing them: 'I will tell you what happened. When people left Kashmir, they left without telling anyone. They never told their neighbours even if their neighbours were also Pandits. One day you will see a family. The next day you see that the windows are shut and there is a heavy padlock on their front door. One by one, families started to leave. When my father saw everyone leaving, he decided that we should leave as well. Like others, we pretended as if it was all fine and left when we felt nobody would be watching.'[27]

While older news reports hinted that a suspected departure was taking place, it was only with the gathering of arriving Pandits in Jammu that a mass displacement (what the Pandits I met would often call 'an exodus' or simply refer to as the 'migration') was noticed. Most conversations with Pandits I had met in Jammu would draw on a common narrative of mass political processions taking place on 19 January 1990 all across Kashmir, where Muslims demanded azaadi. Alongside the different slogans heard at the procession, one slogan that Pandits claim was uttered, which affected them severely, was that azaadi was demanded '*batav bagair, bat nevsan*' (that Pandit men should leave but Pandit women should stay behind). This slogan is mentioned in most accounts and hence flight was seen as a response to a serious threat. Many Muslims deny this slogan and argue that the Pandits were not threatened as a community, while many Pandits insist this threat was made, alongside the publishing of hit lists by militant groups and the selective assassination of prominent Kashmiri Pandits associated with the Indian state.

The Pandits who came to cities such as Jammu found themselves seeking sanctuary in a place unlike their home. The condition of displacement is marked by uncertainty, and the Pandit story is no exception to this. Many had thought that their dislocation was temporary and that they would return to Kashmir once law and order was re-established, though dislocation has become a permanent feature of their lives. Out of 1,40,000 displaced Pandits, approximately 36,000 families were settled in displaced persons camps between 1990–2011 until the replacement of the camps by the township of Jagti. The experience of camp life has been extensively documented by writers including Pandit writers such as Rahul Pandita[28] and Siddhartha Gigoo,[29] who emphasize the sense of alienation they felt in exile, shaped by nostalgia and longing for their home and homeland in Kashmir. In another work I have documented conversations with those who resided in the camps whose testimonies of the early days of displacement attests to a sense of alienation. One man at a camp had this to say: 'Then in 1994, the sarkar [the government] built "pigeon holes" [one-room tenements or ORTs], a *kabutarkhana* in which you cannot even keep buffaloes. The government set up tents in a place where men would be afraid to go alone. When they erected tents here, we saw nothing but snakes and scorpions. We would have to do this every night [he swung his hands and slapped the desk he sat behind to demonstrate]. Snakes would come out of the ground in their thousands. The comfort of the night would be ruined. It was a jungle, all the way to where we are sitting now. When we would go out to urinate, we would take a large stick and lantern . . . This would be around the time of 1990, '91, '94 and '96. The locals would say that a *churel* [witch] lived here. The locals would come here to graze their buffaloes but after sunset, no one would dare to come since the churel will be prowling.'[30]

While Pandit–Muslim relations were marked by complexity in the past, the sense of divide that we imagine within this relationship needs to be interrogated. While Pandits may have felt pride over figures such as Nehru and may not connect to the movement for azaadi in Kashmir, their relationship to politics otherwise is not very clear. Were Pandits ardent Indian nationalists? While organizations from the community such as Panun Kashmir or Roots in Kashmir or old diasporic associations openly support the Indian state and oppose Kashmiri nationalism as 'patriotic Indians', it is difficult to understand how Pandits related to politics in the past. In any case, if the Pandits were not Indian then, the displacement and conflict has made them Indians now. Many political parties often pay lip service to the Pandits, commenting on their suffering. In the Indian public sphere they become a useful case to blunt any criticism of the state if any report of human rights violations in Kashmir are presented. For Hindu nationalism, the Pandits critically provide a group of victims who are upper caste pitted against a movement that all shades of Indian politics, from liberal–secular to Hindu nationalist right wing, see as an Islamist movement.[31]

In the process, the Pandits as a constituent of the Indian nation state have a curious relationship with Indian politics. Many Pandit organizations employ Indian nationalist and Hindu nationalist rhetoric that locate them within India and make them opposed to azaadi. Hence, in my experience, human rights organizations in India which understandably are sympathetic to people in the Valley, often appear to see the Pandits as becoming a constituent of Hindu nationalist and right-wing groups, which is a limited view. The rage of the Pandits at their own conditions at times is directed towards the Muslims of Kashmir and anybody sympathetic to them, which further contributes to their image as an angry people. However, while Hindu nationalists may speak for the Pandits, with the current Indian government claiming it will carry out a series of measures for their benefit, little action appears to be done beyond rhetoric. In my experience, parties such as the BJP and Shiv Sena at the local level represent Hindu Dogra interests. Consequently, the Pandits are often derided by the locals in Jammu for having come to the city, for taking over large parts of the city and for not having 'fought' the Muslims in Kashmir and instead fleeing from Kashmir.

Conversations with Pandits often reveal that they were met with both some hospitality and hostility from the locals when they arrived in cities such as Jammu. A group of youth I had met recalled hearing songs such as: '*Haath mein kangri / kandhe pe jhola / kaha se aye yeh Kashmiri Lola?*' (A brazier in hand/a cloth bag slung on the shoulder/from where have these Kashmiri refugees come?)[32]

All displaced people in Jammu and Kashmir are categorized as 'migrants' by the state and hence are eligible for relief, which comprises financial and food aid. To speak of migrants in Jammu is to speak of the Pandits. The Pandits are not the only displaced people, and many other groups, such as populations fleeing communal conflict in the Pahari areas or border migrants, comprising those who have fled villages around the border due to military action between Indian and Pakistani forces, are also eligible for state assistance. Yet, for some time, it appeared that the Pandits were the most visible group and received a higher corpus of support. Consequently, in areas such as Jammu, the Pandits were seen as a privileged group of victims living off the largesse of the state, unlike others. This connects to the older stereotype of Pandits as elites, which makes any discussion of Pandit suffering difficult. While the displaced often have a difficult relationship in adjusting with locals, the Pandits appear to have an excessive relationship with the Indian nation state with unexpected consequences. While they may have been a religious minority in Kashmir and are part of a religious majority in exile in Jammu or New Delhi, it does not mean that they enjoy entirely cordial relations with other Hindus. As Hindus in a Hindu–majority area, they remain a minority.

Much of the attention of observers of all political shades is in relation to a territory. It is the Kashmir Valley that is converted into a zone of conflict. The people who are living in that zone are treated either as people resisting oppression and suffering state violence or as threats to the Indian state who deserve to be treated with violence. Whether we are looking at Kashmir from the standpoint of political parties of all shades of the political spectrum, the Indian state, Kashmiri nationalist organizations, journalists, social scientists, activists and the larger public, the concern is with the Valley. Anybody outside the Valley, such as the Pandits, is outside our optics and hence somewhat irrelevant and reduced to rhetoric, regardless of our political preferences. However, given the ambiguity of their history and their location in relation to the Kashmir conflict, the Pandits offer a way to understand what being a minority means when it is refracted through histories of socio-economic and political inequality and questions of power. The challenge remains to think about the lives of groups such as the Pandits in relation to concerns of power and history and to yet consider potential futures that acknowledge justice, fairness and voice.

Is There a Future for Urdu?

Mahtab Alam

How often do we hear of the decline, and sometimes even the demise, of Urdu in India? The precarious health of the language, once considered the lingua franca, has been announced from time to time, since at least Partition. The renowned Urdu scholar Shamsur Rahman Faruqi has identified the five years following Partition as 'the worst for Urdu'. In an interview, he reminisces that when he was finishing his high school in 1949, 'students matriculating with Urdu had all but vanished.' The reasons for this, Faruqi says, were firstly obviously 'the wholesale migration of Urdu-medium students and their families to Pakistan', and secondly, and more importantly, the systematic attempt to efface Urdu and replace it with Hindi. Such was the political climate, he recalls, that even those whose first language was Urdu felt compelled to renounce it.[1] The situation improved slightly in the years to come but it could hardly regain its lost position. In the early 1970s, the *New York Times* signposted this anxiety of Urdu lovers noting that parents were advising their children against enrolling in Urdu for fear that it would foreclose career opportunities.[2] Nearly half a century later, things are worse. It is not uncommon to hear a parent's plaint, 'Urdu *parh ke kya karoge?*' (What is the use of studying Urdu?).

Decline of Urdu in North India

Not surprisingly, in the latest census, Gujarati replaced Urdu as the sixth most spoken language of India. The number of Urdu speakers is on a steady decline in north India, especially Uttar Pradesh, which was once considered the bastion of the language, and where protracted and pitched battles over Hindi/Nagari and Urdu/Persian were fought in the early twentieth century. An analysis of the latest census data shows that Uttar Pradesh has 3.85 crore Muslims, but it recorded only 1.08 crore Urdu speakers.[3] In other words, it is not even the primary language of Muslims in Uttar Pradesh because merely 28 per cent Muslims in the state recorded it as such. In other north Indian states such as Madhya Pradesh and Rajasthan, the Urdu speakers are 9.16 lakh and 6.64 lakh respectively. In Bihar, 87.7 lakh Urdu speakers have been enumerated, which is around 50 per cent of the total Muslim population in the state. On the other hand, in Deccan and south Indian states such as Andhra Pradesh, Telangana, Maharashtra and Karnataka, Urdu fares much better. These four states put together account for more than 2.15 crore Urdu speakers, which is almost double the number of Urdu speakers in Uttar Pradesh.

How does one make sense of this decline of Urdu in its erstwhile home, and its comparative fortunes in the south? Discussing the decline of Urdu, former vice president Mohammad Hamid Ansari quoted Dutch sociologist Abram de Swaan, who was of course writing neither in the context of Urdu nor India, but as Ansari found, his insights can be used to understand the fate of Urdu.[4] De Swaan says:

> People who abandon their native tongue do so because they move elsewhere or take up something else and in this new existence they have higher expectations of a different language. Or they neglect it because another language is preferred at school, by public authorities, or in courts of law,

and their own language is treated with disdain. Or they have to stop using it because they are ruled by another nation that imposes its language on them, and, having lost heart, they no longer take care to preserve their own language.

This succinctly explains the decline of Urdu in north India. One may also recall that Urdu had to go through a long legal battle in Uttar Pradesh to attain the status of the second official language of the state. Though given the status of second official language under the Uttar Pradesh Official Language (Amendment) Act, 1989, it was challenged by the Uttar Pradesh Hindi Sahitya Sammelan in 1996, claiming that 'the state government decision had no rationale as there was not much Urdu speaking population in the state'.[5] In September 2014, a Constitution Bench of the Supreme Court dismissed the case and upheld Urdu's status as the second official language of the state, declaring 'there was nothing in Article 345 of the Constitution which bars the state from declaring one or more of the languages in use in the state, in addition to Hindi, as the second official language'.

There can be little doubt that Urdu has been the central trope of identity politics in Uttar Pradesh, and has suffered on this account. But beyond political vicissitudes, there are other reasons which fail to arouse the attention of those sympathetic to the cause of Urdu. Lamentations about the language largely revolve around culture, literature and politics, so much so that over the years Urdu has become synonymous with literature[6] and culture—poetry, fiction and lyrics of Bollywood songs. In other words, a rich language has been reduced to literature and culture, as if it has nothing else to offer other than this. In many ways, more than anything else, this approach has hampered the growth and development of the language, which has the potential as well as history to transcend beyond boundaries of literature and culture. While it is routinely and justly repeated that Urdu is not a language of Muslims alone, it is all too readily forgotten that it is also not the language of shayari, mushairas and lyrics alone.

Unlike Uttar Pradesh then, in states such as Andhra Pradesh, Telangana, Maharashtra and Karnataka, Urdu is a language of utility rather than just novelty. Comparatively, there are more opportunities for Urdu-knowing people. In these states, for a large number of Urdu-speaking communities, it is not just a language of literature but also communication and information. Urdu is not merely taught as another subject, but it is also the medium of education in both primary as well as secondary schools. And these Urdu-medium students after completing their secondary education take up not only Urdu literature and humanities but also pursue medical and engineering courses. One should warn, of course, that the condition of Urdu-medium schools in these states is far from ideal. A comprehensive study of 251 Urdu-medium schools of various levels across Maharashtra presents a dismal picture. It found 127 'single teacher' Urdu-medium schools; further, only 51.5 per cent of the total Urdu medium schools have furniture for all students, and a measly 23.5 per cent of these schools have furniture for some students. Similarly, nearly 9.1 per cent do not have a single functioning toilet seat for boys, while the same for girls is 6.9 per cent. The Maharashtra example is important because it has the largest network of Urdu-medium schools (4900) in the country from primary to the Higher Secondary Certificate (HSC) level. The state also has the largest number of students (approximately 13 lakh) enrolled in Urdu-medium schools in the country.[7]

Can Urdu Regain Its Lost Glory?

The ultimate question then is: Is there a way out? Is there any future of Urdu in India? Or is it condemned to die a slow death, declining year after year? I would say that the crisis or challenge before Urdu is not that of survival but its development and adaptation. We have to think of ways and means to make the Urdu language and literature more communicative, culturally vibrant and relevant. In other words, Urdu will always be there and it will be loved across the country but will it be a language of communication, information and knowledge is the real question before us. Will it survive as a modern language or be reduced to a mere 'dialect' or just being a spoken language? I am of the view that there are limits to which Urdu can be developed and 'revived'. The attempt to regain the 'lost glory of Urdu' is futile at best. There are several reasons for it, theoretical as well as practical. In this regard, Hasan Abdullah has made certain fundamental observations, which need to be reiterated here. Discussing whether Urdu can meet the requirements of a modern language, he notes:

> The answer is both yes and no. In abstraction, the answer would be in the affirmative, because even today there is a sizeable body of people whose mother tongue is Urdu. And, if enough investments are made and these people use their mother tongue for all purposes, except while communicating with the non-Urdu speaking, then—but only then—perhaps, Urdu can meet the requirements of a modern language. But, as anyone can see, that is a hypothetical situation; it is also superfluous.[8]

He further notes, 'Therefore, for all practical purposes, the answer to the question raised above is a definite no. In the above sense, Urdu cannot meet the requirements of a modern language. And English shall remain the language for advanced discourse—particularly in science and technology—because the pace of development in these areas is too fast for a less developed language such as Urdu to bridge the gap and keep the pace.' However, he clarifies that 'it is no aspersion on the language to say that it cannot become a modern language in the above sense'.

According to Abdullah, it only reflects that for the historical reasons, particularly because Urdu was not the favoured language of the powers that be during the rapid development of science and technology, Urdu has lagged behind. Hence, given the present-day realities, it would neither be practical nor prudent to spend energy to bridge this gap completely and keep pace with English.

One might note here that it has not been possible to make Urdu equal to English even in Pakistan, where it enjoys the status of the official language. The same may also be said about Hindi, despite it being the most spoken language in India and the fourth most spoken language in the world. The latest census data reveals that the number of Hindi speakers has grown by more than 25 per cent from the last census (2001), when 41.03 per cent of people spoke Hindi. And yet, it is losing its stature among the millennials. According to a survey conducted by iChamp and published in *India Today*, while most children converse in Hindi with their friends and at home, their skills in writing in the language are surprisingly poor, and they find it difficult to write down words and expressions.[9] Parents too find it challenging to teach them the language and are forced to search for Hindi tutors, the survey reports.

Hence, any strategy to develop and promote Urdu in India should bear the above points in mind. Otherwise, it would be yet another *jazbati* (emotional) approach towards the development and promotion of the language, which has often failed in the past.

What then should be a logical approach to promote and develop Urdu in India? The solution lies in what has been advocated by several linguists, educationists and practitioners: that is, to provide quality primary education in one's mother tongue. In other words, Urdu should be treated as a mother tongue rather than just a language of a religious, cultural or linguistic minority group. There are two components to my proposition: first, primary education should be imparted in one's mother tongue, and secondly, it has to be of high quality, as providing mediocre education in the mother tongue will not solve the problem. The linguist G.N. Devy has noted that while there may be nothing terribly wrong per se in schooling children in the English language, it is scientifically proven that 'education in one's mother tongue gives young learners a far greater ability to grasp complex abstract concepts'.[10]

To illustrate the above point, let me cite a recent example. Sana Niyaz, who topped Delhi in the senior secondary school examination of 2019, told me that she could achieve this because her medium of instruction and examination, and mother tongue were the same, that is, Urdu. Niyaz, a girl from Old Delhi's lower-middle-class family whose father works as a cook in a restaurant and mother is a housewife, achieved this feat without the aid of any coaching classes. When asked if she regretted not choosing English as her medium, she said: 'Had my medium of instruction and examination been English I would not have been able to do this.' She further pointed out that that would not have allowed her the liberty of seeking help from her elder sister and others. One could argue that this is an exception and does not prove that it will always work or has indeed worked in the past. Notably, Niyaz's other sisters have also attended the same Urdu-medium school in the Jama Masjid area, and two years ago, her elder sister Urma scored third position in Delhi.

However, there are other issues involved with Urdu-medium schooling, which is linked to the second part of my proposition, that is, quality education. Due to the lack of quality education in one's mother tongue, especially Urdu, parents are forced to enrol their children in so-called English-medium schools or institutions, where the language of instruction and examination is not the mother tongue of the child. And in these cases, the child faces two problems. First, the child hardly has anyone at home (in most of the cases, if not always) who can provide help in learning the concepts, because they are not comfortable in the medium the child is taught in. Hence, they have to rely on coaching and tuition, which cannot be a viable and long-term substitute for various reasons, including affordability and lack of good tutors. And secondly, and flowing from this, while the child can speak the mother tongue, he or she can't read and write properly, as cited above in the iChamp study, because the focus is on memorizing the concepts of different subjects in an 'alien' language. As a result, in most of the cases, the child ends up becoming language-deficient. The point I am trying to make is that if quality primary education can be provided in one's mother tongue, it can solve the problem of both language proficiency as well as comprehension of the subject. And it is often seen that those who acquire language proficiency at an early stage are likely to contribute more towards the promotion and development of the language.

The Way Forward

Commissioning and publishing quality Urdu translations of good books across genres and languages is another useful mechanism to promote the language. If these were to be made available easily and cheaply, there would surely be enough takers for these texts. There are enough Urdu readers who would prefer reading books in Urdu—an indication of this can be gauged from the figures of readership of Urdu newspapers, which is still growing. A detailed study of the Registrar of Newspapers for India database from 1957–2015 by media watchdog *The Hoot* urges us to look past popular perception. The RNI data shows an increase in both registration of Urdu newspapers and the participation of non-Muslims in the Urdu newspaper industry over the past decade.[11] This would suggest that there are a large number of readers who would like to read books in Urdu as well.

However, there is a complication here and that is that most of the Urdu-knowing people are bilingual and some are indeed trilingual. In fact, Urdu speakers are the most bilingual people in India. As per the latest census data, 62 per cent of Urdu speakers are proficient in two languages and 16 per cent in three languages.[12] And this leads to a situation, as my own experiences both as a reader as well as practitioner inform me, where a large number of Urdu readers can read either Hindi or English. Hence, translating Hindi books and material into Urdu, though easy and cheaper, would not attract much readership as most of them can read them in Hindi. What would be useful is that instead of focusing on translating books into Urdu from Hindi, which is often the case, the focus should be on translating non-Hindi books—Marathi, Telugu, Tamil, Kannada, Bengali and Malayalam—into Urdu. In addition to translating from Indian languages, useful texts from Arabic, Persian and other world languages, apart from English, should be translated into Urdu. All this is important because there is an availability of rich literature in these languages. Moreover, this will also help in bridging the cultural gap, which is very important given the growing segregation of our societies. The translation project will also create and provide job opportunities for Urdu-knowing people along with enriching the language. In doing so, what should be kept in mind is that not just literary and religious books but those of general interest, from politics, sports, cinema to economics, should be translated.

One of the biggest challenges that Urdu-knowing people face is non-availability of Urdu books. They are conspicuously absent in general bookshops and one has to make an extra effort in tracing and procuring Urdu books. Unfortunately, even after the advent and wide reach of digital marketing and outlets such as Amazon, Flipkart, etc., the availability of Urdu books remains a big problem. Besides, most Urdu publishers and distributors lack even a rudimentary understanding of digital marketing and business operations. However, it is slowly picking up and I am told that some new initiatives (such as Kitabdaar.com and UrduBazaar.in) of online marketing and distribution of Urdu books have been receiving a very positive response. However, much more needs to be done on an urgent basis to support Urdu book publishers and distributors with digital marketing and help them to set up and run operations.

In order to publish and promote quality content in Urdu (translations as well as original writing), fellowships and grants must be provided to scholars, researchers and translators. The amounts offered by these fellowships and grants should be such that they can attract talented and competent candidates. In this regard, new themes, subjects and areas of research should be given preference. And one should not shy away from taking help from non-Urdu experts and institutions. In fact, there could be collaborations with different language promotion and development institutions such as those of Marathi, Telugu and Kannada.

Regular readership surveys can reveal the taste and preference of Urdu readers and speakers and can help the Urdu publishing industry in business planning and development. Similarly, special efforts should be made to make Urdu digital-friendly. In this regard, special consultation with different stakeholders (such as software developers, writers, translators, online search engine optimization specialists, etc.) must take place. Since the digital space is an ever-changing field, these exercises should also be of a regular nature. In this regard, Urdu-knowing software developers can play a great role, and fortunately, there are plenty of them around. To begin with, a comprehensive study of existing resources, needs and possible avenues should be carried out.

Role of the Urdu Elite

All this is only possible when the Urdu-knowing elite start taking interest in the development and promotion of the language. Currently, the promotion and development of the language is practically dependent on the economically weaker sections of the society. Largely, if not fully, it has become the language of the deprived and those studying Urdu or in Urdu-medium schools, which is seen as the last resort by those who cannot avail or afford admission elsewhere. This situation can be reversed if the elite start taking a serious interest in Urdu, for example, if they start sending their children to schools that have Urdu as the medium of instruction. In this regard, Sardar Patel Vidyalaya (surely one of the best schools of Delhi) can serve as a model, where the medium of instruction from nursery to class V is Hindi. Similarly, the Urdu elite must start writing on non-literary subjects (not just politics and social issues but also science and economics) in Urdu. Only whining about the sorry state of public discourse in Urdu is not going to help. All this will lead to two things: firstly, it will improve the quality of education of Urdu-medium schools and discourse in the language. And secondly, it will force the government to take Urdu more seriously because a combination of masses and elites can certainly work as a pressure group to ensure that Urdu is not being sidelined.

The role of the government and its agencies is very crucial because both the promotion as well as development of the language require capital investment and human resources. To begin with, there must be pressure put on the government to fill all the vacant positions of teachers in Urdu-medium schools or Urdu teachers in other schools. Secondly, the government ought to provide training and basic infrastructural facilities to Urdu teachers, which are lacking in most of the cases across India. Similarly, the state governments need to set up an 'Institute of Urdu', as suggested by Abdul Shaban in his study of Urdu-medium schools in Maharashtra. The institute should be expressly devoted to the promotion of research and teaching of secular subjects in the Urdu language. Such an institute could go a long way in creating a cadre of 'trained people who would help in strengthening the Urdu medium school syllabus, produce technical vocabularies for Urdu and textbooks in Urdu language required at school and higher level of learnings'.[13] Unfortunately, institutions such as the National Council for Promotion of Urdu Language and state Urdu academies are either not doing this or are not in a position to meet these objectives. Therefore, a regular social audit of these institutions should be carried out.

In short, the promotion and development of Urdu in the current scenario would require a multifaceted, long-term and planned approach straddling education, research, digital advancement, cultural activities, to making it a language of day-to-day use. Any effort devoid of a comprehensive approach is bound to fail as we have seen in the past. The future of Urdu lies in moving ahead with time, not just thinking about its glorious past.

Education and the Muslim Child

Azra Razzack and Muzna F. Alvi

In my childhood, the most significant event that played a major part in my determining the Muslim position in India was one that occurred at the level of fantasy. A persisting and nerve-racking thought that would often obsess me was that if I was ever to get lost somewhere or if I happened to be kidnapped and if my rescuers/kidnappers demanded to know my name, what would I reply? Would it be my own name which cried out in no uncertain terms that I was a Muslim, or would I for the moment concoct a new name which would not give away my Muslim identity? . . .

The fear of 'sadhus' and 'mandirs' did not, however, prevent me from attempting to be part of the larger social group to which my classmates belonged. Trying eagerly to find tulsi leaves in the school bushes along with my friends during examination days (they said keeping tulsi leaves on one's tongue through the duration of the exam would help in doing better) and holding out both my hands, palm upwards, for prasad (I was told that was the correct way) which a friend may have got to school was the best I could do at that time to bridge the hiatus between me and my classmates. But this was all in vain because I was always perceived by my friends and classmates as being different. The crucial part of my growing up Muslim was to learn to see that I was different from my peer group.[1]

Introduction

India's young population is often touted as its biggest asset. Compared to other socio-religious groups in India, Muslims have the highest share of population in the 0–19 years age group according to the 2011 Census data. Education is one of the most pressing issues concerning this age group, and by extension, the Muslim community. Educational backwardness of Indian Muslims is a much talked about fact, and varying perceptions regarding its cause persist. These range from poverty, lack of inclination towards modern education and preference for madrasa education, to cultural ethos, systemic discrimination and treatment of girls, among others. The criticality of this also needs to be recognized in light of prevailing stereotypes concerning the Muslim community. The skewed perceptions about Muslims contribute to the strengthening of such distortions. The lack of an informed leadership too has been problematic for the community as Muslim issues tend to be seen from the lens of identity alone. Eventually, this results in their life experiences being screened out of public discourse.

In 2006 the Sachar Committee presented substantial data on the education status of India's Muslims, putting to rest several arguments of community appeasement that had dominated discussion until then. On many indicators, the Muslim community was shown to be placed alongside Scheduled Castes and Scheduled Tribes and, in some respects, was even worse off than them.[2] However, data alone does not tell us the exact story, nor does it allow us to see the inherent inconsistencies. Mere statistics cannot provide answers nor inform policy, especially for education. Therefore, to understand and address the issues of education of the Muslims in India, it is imperative to understand both challenges and opportunities presented by existing internal and external power structures and the complicated sociopolitical history of Indian Muslims that continues to affect educational outcomes for the community.

The years following Independence were critical as they set the agenda for a new nation in the making. India was left with a substantial Muslim population and a Hindu majority. Education was one of the critical means by which the desire to bring about a secular and democratic society was to be enacted. While India declared itself to be a secular state and as being above religious differences, there were some who were unwilling to tolerate any concessions to Muslims, whom they held responsible for the partition of the country.[3] However, the architects of the Indian Constitution took care to ensure that becoming Indian citizens on an equal footing did not in any way challenge people's affiliations to their respective identities. Caste-based reservation to take care of the years of social discrimination experienced by Dalits and tribals was put into place. Linguistic re-organization of states was done to satisfy the demands of exclusive language groups. The Constitution also guaranteed the safeguarding of religious and cultural identities. Additionally, with this immense diversity of cultures and religions, under Article 30 of the Constitution, it was decided that India would provide its minorities a right to establish and administer educational institutions of their choice and through this secure a protection of their identity. Apart from this passive measure, no explicit provisions were made to actively promote the participation of religious minorities in mainstream non-denominational educational institutions.

With this background, a relevant question that arises is: What has been on offer for the Muslim community in this independent and diverse India? How has the community shaped itself and responded to the education on offer? This is a huge challenge. Given that the Constitution gave minority communities the right to establish their institutions, and in doing so choose the education for their children, what in reality have been the choices available to the community?

Threat of 'cultural extermination' and concern for preservation of its identity was a matter of great concern for Muslims immediately following Partition.[4] They turned towards the innumerable maktabs and madrasas which had spread in the early decades after Independence. There was a sudden and rapid increase in the number of madrasas in Uttar Pradesh and Bihar as well as an increase in the number of students enrolled.[5] This is significant because a large number of the Muslim population had migrated to Pakistan. According to M. Mujeeb:

> The upsurge of self-consciousness in the majority community . . . has created the fear that it will take advantage of its numerical preponderance to modify the secularism of the state and also reduce the cultural identity of the Muslims to something negligible if not meaningless. There is, for this reason, a growing realization among the Indian Muslims that they must organize the religious education of their children and illiterate adults to counteract what appear to be the anti-Islamic tendencies of education in government schools, as well as the increasing general indifference to religious and moral values.[6]

Though providing for secular and modern education has been a part of the Muslim discourse since Independence, efforts towards this started only in the 1970s and gained momentum in the decades after. In post-liberalization India, the discourse, at least within the community, shifted. Questions were raised on the ways in which the current educational choices available to Muslim children and youth could enable them to participate and gain from a rapidly expanding economy.

How has the issue of diversity and national identity been discussed in the educational discourse? What have been the implications of this on minorities in India over the last seven decades? To what extent has India's affirmation of its pluralist character informed its discourse around education and the process of schooling? Given that the Constitution has given minority communities the right regarding the education of their children, what discourses has this given rise to within the communities? Answers to each of these questions are critical to understanding how the narrative around education and schooling in post-Independence India enables diversity, pluralism and inclusion.

Educational Discourse and Indian Muslims

The educational discourse in contemporary India, until very recently, has been particularly rigid, allowing virtually no space for diversity and exalting the notion of a single Indian identity. Differences based on language, religion, region and caste were seen as undesirable and considered to be the cause of divisiveness. The discourse maintained that no space should be given to these 'narrow' and 'petty' loyalties unless we want to forget the singular Indian identity. It is these 'selfish' loyalties which give rise to divisive forces, thus disturbing the country and weakens the feeling of national solidarity. This 'dangerous gulf', the discourse maintains, had to be bridged and it was the responsibility of education to overcome these dividing forces.[7] Education was to be used as a tool for the realization of 'national goals', 'national aspirations' and meeting 'national challenges' and through it would come individual fulfilment.[8] Education and schooling were thus held sacred in the discourse as a powerful mechanism for creating national uniformity among the heterogenous groups within Indian society. Analysis of school textbooks also highlights their largely mono-cultural orientation.[9]

While education has been the arena where the notion of Indian identity has been in the forefront, its role in actively supporting and promoting a plural and multicultural society has been negligible.

Recognition of this diversity and emphasis on pluralism is a relatively new chapter in the Indian educational discourse since the mid-2000s. The National Curriculum Framework (NCF) of 2005 reflected this shift by making the child its focus rather than the nation. It was around this time that the Sachar Committee too was set up to look at the social, economic and educational status of Muslims in India. In 2005 the Centre for Dalit and Minorities Studies was established in Jamia Millia Islamia, marking the first time such a centre was set up in a central university. Many such centres were to follow in universities across the country, bringing to focus formal and rigorous studies of India's marginalized communities. The discourse clearly was changing with inclusion becoming the focus, including in India's Twelfth Five Year Plan document. In January 2006, the Ministry of Minority Affairs was carved out of the Ministry of Social Justice and Empowerment, formalizing the Centre's recognition of social and economic exclusion faced by India's religious minorities. This shift in discourse thus recognized India's plurality not as a threat to national identity, rather as central to maintaining India as a nation.

The draft 2019 New Education Policy also mentions certain explicit measures for underrepresented groups, which include Muslims. The policy also gives space to *the regional and the local*, something which the earlier committees and commissions on education were not inclined to do, referring to them as fissiparous tendencies. The draft also talks of interventions to incentivize Muslims and other educationally underrepresented minorities to complete school education and of providing 'excellent schools' in areas where the Muslim population is high. Besides this, the policy talks of other interventions which will help Muslim children enter higher education: bridging of language barriers, scholarships, movement of students from madrasas into higher education by being allowed to appear for state board examinations and assessment by the National Testing Agency (NTA). Recruitment of teachers from underrepresented groups is also highlighted as an inclusive policy. How this policy will be translated to action remains to be seen.

Debating Education, Deprivation and Backwardness

Problems faced by Muslims in accessing education are manifold. Muslims face cumulative deprivation—of belonging to a minority group, of being Muslim, of being poor, of being uneducated, and so on. While physical access to schools has improved over the years and there exist special government and community initiatives, many Muslim children continue to remain educationally marginalized. The Sachar Committee Report placed before the Indian Parliament important data. The relative deprivation of Muslims in education was very clear. On nearly all indicators Muslims fared poorly, be it literacy, school enrolment, dropout rates or higher secondary attainments levels.

Low level of education attainment is worrisome, especially since it is correlated with higher incidence of poverty and child labour, both of which are high among Muslims compared to other socio-religious categories (SRCs), except for SCs/STs. Additionally, the necessary support from home for the schoolgoing child is absent for the Muslim child because of parental illiteracy as well as inability to provide for high-quality tuitions, which have become such an essential part of today's educational system. This is exacerbated because of low perceived returns from education, as most Muslims are in self-employment where returns to education are not directly observed and unemployment rates for Muslims are the highest across all SRCs. Apart from this is the fact that access to schools too is poor and there is either a lack of good-quality schools in Muslim areas or a lack of hostel facilities where good schools do exist. Shortage of schools in the vicinity particularly hampers girls' schooling. The content of school textbooks as well as the school ethos are some of the other factors that come in the way of education for the Muslim child. Added to this is the experience of discrimination and marginalization faced by students.[10]

Even today, despite there being enough evidence of Muslim educational backwardness, the state's response has remained limited. Schemes for the modernization of madrasas or the reiteration of the provision of Article 30 of the Constitution seem to be the only response on offer. Post-Sachar, the government initiated a number of schemes for madrasa modernization, despite the report showing that less than 5 per cent Muslim children attend madrasas. Well intentioned as they may be, these initiatives are widely perceived within the community as being tokenistic and not being contextualized to better meet the needs of the Muslim community. While allowing the community to set up educational institutions of its choice, the state abdicates its own responsibility and places the onus on the community itself. Education, surely, has been a contested terrain.

Minority Educational Institutions, Madrasas and Schooling

Article 30 of the Constitution of India has provided space to minorities within the country to establish educational institutions of their choice. As a result, we find that over the last seven decades this has been a constitutional provision which has been drawn upon by the Muslim community, as well as the state, on a near-continuous basis. Muslims have relied upon this Article to set up madrasas or regular modern educational institutions. On the other hand, a curious fallout of this provision of the Constitution has been that the response to the educational backwardness of the Muslims, as stated earlier, has mostly led to attention being drawn only to community-led educational institutions, while glossing over the government's failure in setting up quality schools and colleges in Muslim areas, or increasing Muslim children's access to such institutions. That both these largely concern the community's own initiative was never ever highlighted, with the Muslim community itself lapping it up as a major concession granted to them.

One also needs to remember that while the setting up of denominational institutions is a right given to minorities under Article 30 of the Constitution, it was not meant to become the only option available to them. While Article 30 has indeed provided opportunities for education, this clause has also contributed to building a sense of false comfort for the community. It has also resulted in taking Muslims out of a mode of healthy competition, a hallmark of quality government institutions. The Muslim community while clinging on desperately to this constitutional provision has unwittingly limited the choice for its own children.

The announcement of the new incarnation of the 'madrasa modernization scheme', Scheme to Provide Quality Education in Madrasas (SPQEM), in 2009, was sufficient to excite the community and to draw applause. Exercising Article 30 allows the community to believe that they have achieved success. Similarly, giving Jamia Millia Islamia the status of a 'minority' institution in 2011 was met with huge celebrations. The Sachar Committee had recommended that educational institutions be set up in minority concentration areas. In an almost knee-jerk reaction, the Manmohan Singh government brought into action this important recommendation of the Sachar Committee Report—it gave Muslims an educational institution right at their doorstep, without any actual resource investment! Muslim-dominated neighbourhoods of Delhi like Batla House, Noor Nagar, Zakir Nagar were now blessed with a 'minority' institution of higher education at a walking distance. Through this judgment, Muslims were discreetly told that they could continue to remain confined in their own worlds, believing that they have achieved distinction, or better still, that distinction does not matter, only the 'minority' tag does.

Sections of the Muslim community were intoxicated with this judgment without fully realizing what its implications are for the community. Unfortunately, Muslims once again got trapped. The government managed to deceive Muslims into believing that they have acquired a goldmine! Through this judgment, Jamia Millia Islamia, which for all practical purposes was serving the educational interests of the Muslim community for the last ninety years, was now gifted back to them with a minority tag. The moot question was, how would a few additional seats in an otherwise 'Muslim' university help Muslim educational backwardness? What additional benefit would this judgment have for the community—other than a sense of comfort and an imagined and false sense of well-being? Why is this a matter of concern? The cost of setting up any new secular government institution of higher learning in a Muslim concentration area would run into thousands of crores. By one stroke, this judgment managed to save government huge funds while getting it unwarranted political mileage.

However, this provision of the Constitution is not without its share of controversies. Despite Article 30 and authoritative pronouncements by the Supreme Court, rights of minority institutions are routinely contested. There are innumerable cases in the courts where minority institutions have been fighting for their right to independent governance. Directorates of education in many states across the country pose hindrances in the functioning of minority educational institutions. The issue becomes especially cumbersome when such minority institutions are aided by public funds. As an example, often the directorate of education insists that the constitutional reservations of Scheduled Castes/Scheduled Tribes should be applied in minority schools as well, including in matters of employment. On the other hand, a 2010 judgment of the Supreme Court in the Sindhi Education Society's case (8 SCC 49) states that the provision of SC/ST reservations as a pre-condition for release of aid/funds by the state cannot be applied to minority schools.

An emerging concern is the enactment of the new Right to Education Act (RTE), and its exclusion of minority institutions from its purview. That the entire Act has been made inapplicable to minority institutions means that a compulsory government mandate has been taken away. By keeping minority institutions out of the ambit of RTE, Muslim children are being deprived of quality education. All provisions that come into play while providing for the education of India's children should clearly be applicable to Muslim children as well. If providing schools is a function of the state, surely the state should also play a role in their assessment. Article 30 gives minorities the right to set up their own educational institutions, however, in no way does it condone the right to maladminister nor gives institutions the right to be protected from scrutiny. Right to manage should not mean right to mismanage. By taking advantage of Article 30, a select group of powerful elites from the community is creating a monopoly over management of educational institutions, without any institutional or statutory checks and balances. This is clearly not in the interest of the minorities themselves and will be detrimental to the interest of the students and by extension to their right to quality education. That RTE should not apply to minorities is thus prejudicial to their interest.

Article 30 of the Constitution has put the community in a strange bind. While it seems to have empowered the community, allowing them to set up institutions of their 'own choice', over the years it has become the only source through which Muslims have been able to access education, be it schools, madrasas, professional colleges or institutions of higher learning. The exorbitant fee demanded by many of these institutions also places Muslim children from a modest background at a disadvantage. All of this combines to mean that Muslim youth enter the job market with degrees from institutions that have a 'minority' tag and are often seen as inferior to more secular institutions. Moreover, lack of statutory oversight at these institutions means that often the quality of education received at these institutions is deficient in meeting the needs of a modern economy.

It is pertinent to note that most Muslims no longer want madrasa education for their children as is routinely suggested. Muslims in India aspire for their children to have quality secular education while meeting the identity needs of the community. In response to the formation of the Rajasthan Madrasa Board in 2003, Syed

Shahabuddin, a well-known spokesperson for the community, wrote to the then chief minister of Rajasthan:

> Won't it be better if your government opened regular schools in the deprived areas so that the Muslim children may have normal education? Why should your government deliberately consign Muslim children to madrasas and madrasas only?
>
> My view is that even with so-called modernization the madrasas cannot be equivalent of normal schools. Therefore, this approach is discriminatory. My view also is that the 'modernized madrasas' will not be proper madrasas either.
>
> . . . the steps your government has taken are populist and election-oriented. The government may gain a set of supporters in the teachers, if their salaries are paid by the madrasa board. But they are fraught with grave consequences for the institutions of madrasa.
>
> I once again request you to instruct the Department of Education to establish government schools in accordance with national norms. [11]

Referring to the educational efforts made after the riots of 2002, sociologist Dipankar Gupta noted that Islamic relief organizations 'do not seek to set up madrasas to address the need for education among Muslim riot survivors, but secular schools that follow the state educational board, thus reaffirming their desire to be considered legitimate citizens of the nation state even though the same state has committed gross injustices upon their community'. There is now an assertion for secular institutions where along with the regular curriculum children can also learn about their traditions: 'What emerges through these multiple—and not always contradictory—visions and ideals is the forging of transformed citizenship models, possessing potential for greater inclusion, participation and diversity.'[12]

Education and Muslims in Contemporary Times

Given that a vast majority of Muslim children are attending regular educational institutions and not madrasas, it is also necessary to reflect on what challenges and constraints are faced by these students in accessing mainstream education, and what opportunities are available for them once they graduate from these institutions.[13] As discussed previously, overall, the level of literacy among Muslims is only marginally better than that of SCs/STs, and much worse than Other Backward Classes,[14] all of whom are constitutionally protected groups. Even though in recent times India has ensured near-universal primary school enrolment, data suggests that Muslim children are much more likely to drop out of school at all terminal levels: primary, middle, secondary or higher education. Less than 87 per cent Muslim children in the six-to-fourteen-year-old category are currently attending school, compared to 95 per cent upper-caste Hindus and 91 per cent SCs/STs, and this rift widens at progressively higher age categories. Unlike SCs/STs, Muslim youth do not have access to reservation in government colleges and universities, which are not only known for providing high-quality education but are also heavily subsidized by the government. In the absence of access to affordable and quality higher education, the incentive for Muslim children to remain in school is significantly depressed.

The average dropout age for Muslim children is a full year lower than that for Hindus, therefore, Muslim children have completed fewer years of education at the time of dropout than others. These youth are thus entering the labour market not only with lower social capital due to their disadvantaged status as minorities, but also with lower human capital, that severely restricts the job opportunities available to them. The question then is, when and why are Muslim children dropping out of schools? Studying the reasons for withdrawal of children from formal education can provide policymakers with potential entry points to ensure that policies address the specific constraints faced by the community.

Financial constraint is stated as the single most important reason for the dropping out of Muslim children. This constraint potentially works in two ways: first, Muslim parents are poorer and thus less able to spend on their children's education, and second, Muslims are much more likely to attend more expensive, but lower quality, private institutions due to access issues.

All this might lead one to believe that Muslim parents do not invest or see value in investing in their children's education. However, evidence suggests that Muslims spend more, in proportionate terms, on private coaching compared to every SRC. Muslim children are also much more likely to avail private coaching, primarily to supplement lower-quality education received in schools. Investments are thus being made by parents to bridge the gap between the quality of education being offered in school, and the quality they aspire to.

The modern Muslim is seeking education that equips them with the skills needed to participate in a rapidly globalizing and integrated economy. Despite shortcomings, the community has made efforts in this regard by setting up minority educational institutions. Parents too are making investments in ensuring their children get the education they need to succeed. It is now imperative on the government to meet the needs of the community's youth and children by expanding the availability of government educational institutions.

Conclusion

In trying to consolidate an understanding of the education of Indian Muslims since Independence, one realizes the enormity of the task at hand. Various actors are at play: state, community, individuals; various dimensions need to be looked at: social, political and economic; and despite this, popular discourse, research and attention seems to stop with only presenting data on Muslims. While data is helpful in highlighting the extent of deprivation, serious attention to the specificities is barely visible.

Desire for schooling and accessibility of schooling seems to be not so much of a problem today in India. Article 30 too has ensured that many schools have been made available for the community. While the initial years after Independence did not see much of a growth, the Gulf boom helped do a turnaround. Today, there is a proliferation of schools being run by the community. Added to this are the madrasas which have flourished. The SPQEM scheme too provided an impetus with many small teaching shops calling themselves madrasas opening up to avail of benefits being provided by the MHRD.

What does all of this say about the schooling of Muslim children? Comparative studies on minorities seem to suggest that differences in academic achievement of minorities cannot only be explained by societal and school factors alone, or what can be referred to as systemic factors. Rather 'community factors' too needed to be taken into account if the academic gap is to be understood. The interplay of various forces from within the community which can affect the smooth functioning of a school is also worth noting.[15] With stakeholders of the community vying with each other to take on the reins of education, we need to ask what exactly is on offer. We also need to assess the issues located within the community that may hinder the progress of educational institutions as well as the issues located within the family and within the intra world of the school. Mere lamentation about communal attitudes and discrimination will not take the community far. The question needs to be asked, has the provision of Article 30 benefited the community, and if yes to what extent? How has it helped the community distance itself from the larger social world? How has this ghettoization helped in the growth of interpersonal relations? The interplay of external forces and the school is yet another dimension.

Instead of opening more quality schools in Muslim concentration areas and making schools sensitive to the needs of the Muslim community, successive state and central governments it seems are keen to cash in on the available resource of the community itself by providing it with some sops in the name of a small grant or else providing for language, math and science teachers on reduced salaries.[16] The SPQEM was initiated in 2009 by the Ministry of Human Resource Development (MHRD). This is a demand-driven scheme. The basic features of this scheme provide for extending support and capacity building of madrasas to teach modern subjects. Financial assistance is provided for teachers' salaries, strengthening of libraries and book banks, providing teaching learning materials and so on. Assistance is also provided for the establishment of science and computer labs. There is also provision in the scheme for in-service training for teachers. However, one finds that despite there being a great demand for this scheme, there are many issues of concern. The amount given for salaries for teachers is minimal at Rs 6000 and Rs 12,000. There are huge delays in disbursing funds; at times teachers have not got their salaries for more than two years. There is no concept of increment to be given to teachers. This is rather surprising considering the fact that the name of the scheme has the word quality included in it. How can teachers deliver quality with low salaries and that too received after long delays is anyone's guess.[17]

The regular announcement of some scheme or the other is an attempt at conveying that the problems of schooling will now be over, especially for those who have been hitherto deprived of schooling and the opportunities it offers. No effort is made towards understanding the real issues in the schooling of Muslim children. In a powerful piece in *EPW* titled 'I, a Manual Scavenger, Not Your Vote Bank', a research scholar of Delhi University has written:

> They keep coming up with different schemes and committees to show how inclusive they are . . . They are afraid that if I become aware of my politico-cultural positioning in society, I may begin to reason between good and bad, right and wrong,

logical and illogical, pure and impure, equality and inequality,
sacred and secular and, more importantly, whom I should
vote for, for my emancipation. They are afraid that I may start
questioning why, after being loyal to one political party since
independence, I am still being subjected to the same kind
of work. In this ram rajya, I am expected to remain happy
with the work 'fate' has assigned to me—manual scavenging.
Simply put, I hate being stuck in this murkiness. I hate being
trapped in the web of brahmanical ideology. This is like
marshy land—the more I try to scramble out of it, the more
I find myself getting sucked in by the bog.[18]

How true this is for the Muslim community as well!

The widening socio-economic differentials, especially at
high levels of education, draw attention to the thesis propounded
by cultural reproduction theorists like Bourdieu, Bowles and
Gintis who have argued that 'since educational certificates serve
gatekeeping functions for access to high prestige jobs, educational
system devised by the elites often contain many hurdles to exclude
the subordinate groups from higher education'.[19] According to
Sonalde Desai and Veena Kulkarni, 'perhaps the most ironic finding
in this line of research is that even in communist societies, cultural
capital reflected in father's educational level increased children's
chances of gaining higher education'.[20]

The change in the way madrasas are being viewed in India
today is curious. While the stereotype of madrasas as a den of
terrorism continues to persist and is a cause of grave distress to the
community, recognition of their existence as a potential resource to
fulfil the state's agenda of improving literacy levels in the country,
as well as fulfilling the constitutional obligation of providing for
compulsory education for all children up to the elementary levels of
schooling has gained ground. The government is willingly utilizing
this resource of the community to meet its own target of providing
for elementary education. It is thus apparent that the luxury of real

education, as is on offer for other children in India, is not available for the Muslim child. They have to manage their life with 'modern madrasas', skill development and vocational courses. Becoming graduates, post-graduates and aspiring to get into white-collar jobs seems to be a remote possibility. Insistence on madrasa intervention as a remedy for Muslim educational backwardness, therefore, appears to be designed for disappointment.

References

Alvi, Muzna. *Essays in the Economics of Caste and Religion*, PhD dissertation. Michigan State University, 2012.

Guha, Ramachandra. *India after Gandhi: The History of the World's Largest Democracy*, pp. xvi–xvii.

Notes

Introduction

1. L.K. Advani, 'Dr Munshi's Historic Letter to Pandit Nehru: VP Menon Calls It "a Masterpiece"', *Times of India*, 11 October 2013, https://timesofindia.indiatimes.com/blogs/lkadvanis-blog/dr-munshi-s-historic-letter-to-pandit-nehru-vp-menon-calls-it-a-masterpiece.

2. Ibid.

3. The Indic/non-Indic dichotomy is often also deployed by anthropologists of religions, Indologists, Orientalists and theologians to classify religious persuasions on the basis of their place of birth.

4. Balraj Madhok, *Indianisation* (Delhi: Hind Pocket Books, 1970).

5. Tara Chand, *Influence of Islam on Indian Culture* (Allahabad: Indian Press, 1936), p. 137.

6. Ashis Nandy, 'Politics of Secularism and the Recovery of Religious Tolerance', *Alternatives*, XIII (1988): 177–94.

7. Presidential Address of Jinnah, Lahore, March 1940, in Jamil-ud-din Ahmad, ed., *Speeches and Writings of Mr. Jinnah, Vol. I*, Lahore, S.M. Ashraf (1960, sixth edition), p. 162.

8. *State of UP v. Anjuman Madrasa Noorul Islam Dehra Kala and Others*, in High Court of Allahabad, Special Appeal Defective No. 322

of 2007, Rd–Ah 6384, April 6, 2007 https://indiankanoon.org/doc/9615.

9. https://main.sci.gov.in/jonew/judis/551.pdf.
10. *T.M.A. Pai Foundation and Others v. State of Karnataka and Others,* https://main.sci.gov.in/jonew/judis/18737.pdf.
11. Irfan Ahmad and Santosh Mehrotra, 'No Respite from Poverty for Muslims', *The Hindu,* 6 November 2018, https://www.thehindu.com/opinion/op-ed/no-respite-from-poverty-for-muslims/article25429598.ece.
12. David Runciman, *How Democracy Ends* (New York: Basic Books, 2018).

Disenfranchised Minorities, Dysfunctional Democracies

1. See Plato, *The Republic,* trans. Desmond Lee (Penguin Classics, 1996), Book IX.
2. Mark Chou, 'Sowing the Seeds of Its Own Destruction: Democracy and Democide in the Weimar Republic and Beyond', *Theoria: A Journal of Social and Political Theory* 59.133 (December 2012): 21–49.
3. Timothy Mitchell, *Carbon Democracy: Political Power in the Age of Oil* (London: Verso, 2011).
4. Matthew Weaver, 'Timeline: Donald Trump's Feud with Sadiq Khan', *Guardian,* 15 June, 2019.
5. Susan Cornwell and Richard Cowan, 'U.S. House Condemns Trump over "Racist Comments" Tweeted at Congresswomen', Reuters, 15 July 2019, https://in.reuters.com.
6. Steven Levitsky and Daniel Ziblatt, *How Democracies Die: What History Reveals about Our Future* (New York: Penguin, 2018), p. 57.
7. Javed M. Ansari, 'Making Hate So Normal: The BJP fielding Pragya Thakur Is an Attempt to Mainstream Terror Accused Persons. Our Silence Is Criminal', DailyO, 24 April 2019. See also Kumar Anshuman, 'Pragya Thakur Only Talks about Hindu, Muslim, Mandir; That Isn't NDA Agenda: KC Tyagi, *Economic Times,* 22 April 2019.

8. Sumana Ramanam, 'Film-maker Releases a Dozen Clips of Controversial Modi Speeches Made Just after Gujarat Riots: Rakesh Sharma Aims to Show How Modi's Image Is Being Whitewashed', Scroll, 10 March 2014, https://scroll.in/article/658119.

9. Vandana, 'Hate Is Hate, Mr. Owaisi: Akbaruddin Owaisi Is a Repeat Hate Speech Offender. Why Should Different Standards Apply?' DailyO, 1 August 2019.

10. Sammy Smooha, 'The Model of Ethnic Democracy: Israel as a Jewish and Democratic State', Nations and Nationalism 8.4, https://doi.org/10/1111/1469-8219.00062

11. Victoria Gagliardo-Silver, 'Facebook Bans Artist after She Posted Swastika Made of Make America Great Again (MAGA) Hats, Independent, 26 May 2019.

12. John Blundell, 'Thatcher Put "Great" in Great Britain', USA Today, 9 April 2013, https://www.usatoday.com.

13. Bob Jessop, Kevin Bonnett, Simon Bromley and Tom Ling, Thatcherism: A Tale of Two Nations (Cambridge: Polity Press, 1988).

14. Wilhelm Reich, The Mass Psychology of Fascism (New Delhi: Aakar Books Classics, 2013).

15. Jacques Semelin, Purify and Destroy: The Political Uses of Massacre and Genocide (London: Hurst & Company, 2013), p. 365.

16. Hannah Arendt, Eichmann in Jerusalem: A Report on the Banality of Evil (Penguin Modern Classics, 2006).

Bearing Witness: Living in Times of Hate

1. The author wishes to express her sincere gratitude to Harsh Mander and his Karwan-e-Mohabbat comrades for leading and continuing the Karwan.

2. Bengali Muslims were targeted in the Nellie massacre in Assam in 1983 where during a six-hour period more than 2000 Bengali Muslims whose ancestors had relocated in pre-Partition British India were massacred in cold blood. Sikhs became the target of brutal attacks in 1984 in Delhi and other cities following the killing of the then prime minister Indira Gandhi by her security

guards who happened to be Sikh. In Hashimpura in 1987, during a Hindu–Muslim communal riot in Meerut, the Provincial Armed Constabulary personnel rounded up forty-two Muslim youths and shot them in cold blood and dumped their bodies in a nearby irrigation canal. In 1989, in the wake of the Ram Janmabhoomi campaign led by the Hindu right, Bhagalpur was rocked by major violence which spread to rural areas, in what is known as the first large-scale rural riot, and Muslims faced mass violence. Muslims were once again under attack in Mumbai in 1992–93 in the aftermath of the Babri mosque demolition, and in 2002 again, in the aftermath of the Godhra tragedy, Muslims in Gujarat faced unprecedented large-scale violence, including sexual violence. Christians were targets of attacks in southern Karnataka in 2008 when churches and prayer halls were desecrated. Again in 2008 in Kandhamal, Odisha, dozens of Christians were killed and thousands lost homes. It was Muslims again in Muzaffarnagar in 2013, to name only a few major-scale episodes of violence.

3. The Hate Crime Tracker site was taken down on 12 September 2019. The original data was created in collaboration with the Karwan-e-Mohabbat initiative, as a result of which we have access to the raw data files.

4. Harsh Mander, 'New Hate Crime Tracker in India Finds Victims Are Predominantly Muslims, Perpetrators Hindus', Scroll, 2018, https://scroll.in/article/901206/new-hate-crime-tracker-in-india-finds-victims-are-predominantly-muslims-perpetrators-hindus (accessed 22 November 2019).

5. A. Kumar, 'The Lynching that Changed India', Al Jazeera, 2017, https://www.aljazeera.com/indepth/features/2017/09/lynching-changed-india-170927084018325.html (accessed 22 November 2019).

6. https://indianexpress.com/article/india/india-others/madhya-pradesh-man-kills-friends-over-cow-slaughter-held (accessed 2 December 2019).

7. https://www.thehindu.com/news/national/other-states/accused-in-lynching-of-man-in-rajasthan-still-remain-free/article7830070.ece (accessed 2 December 2019).

8. *Times of India*, 'Attacks on Muslims since Mohammed Akhlaq's Lynching: A Timeline', 2017, https://timesofindia.indiatimes. com/india/attacks-on-muslims-since-mohammed-akhlaqs-lynching-a-timeline/articleshow/61778337.cms (accessed 22 November 2019).

9. D. Sethi, 'Cow Lynching Timeline: Steady Increase under BJP with a Spike in 2017', *Citizen*, 2017, https://www.thecitizen. in/index.php/en/NewsDetail/index/1/12005/Cow-Lynching-Timeline-Steady-Increase-Under-BJP-With-A-Spike-in-2017 (accessed 22 November 2019).

10. Days after Akhlaque's killing, on 6 October in Karkala, Udupi, Karnataka, a cattle-trader, Ibrahim Padubidri, was attacked by a mob of alleged Bajrang Dal activists based on a rumour about a stolen cow. On 9 October, in Karhal, Mainpuri, Uttar Pradesh, two young people, Rafeeq and Habib, were badly beaten up on the basis of a cow slaughter rumour; on 14 October, in Sirmaur, Himachal Pradesh, vigilantes killed Mohammad Noman and injured several others for the alleged smuggling of a truckload of cattle. Next was Zahid Ahmad Bhat, who was lynched by a mob in Udhampur in Jammu and Kashmir on 18 October; on 19 October, Jammu and Kashmir MLA engineer Rashid was thrashed for holding a beef party in Srinagar; on 9 December, a migrant worker, Khush Noor, was lynched by a cow vigilante group in Bhanukheri village in Karnal, Haryana. This timeline was recorded on the IndiaSpend website by the Hate Crime Tracker. It has since then been taken down. The original data was created in collaboration with the Karwan-e-Mohabbat initiative, as a result of which we have access to the files and are thus using it as a reference for recordings of instances of hate crimes in India.

11. On 18 March 2016, in Latehar, Jharkhand, gau rakshaks (cow vigilantes) killed cattle-trader Mazloom and a twelve-year-old boy, Imtiaz Khan, on the suspicion of stealing cattle. They were executed by hanging.

12. This data was taken from the IndiaSpend Hate Crime Tracker.

13. Ibid.

14. https://www.bbc.com/news/world-asia-india-40393331.

15. https://www.bbc.com/news/world-asia-india-39769172.

16. T. Anwar , 'Latehar Lynching: Eight Convicted for Handing Two Muslims to Death, Key Accused Still at Large', Newsclick, 2018, https://www.newsclick.in/latehar-lynching-eight-convicted-hanging-two-muslims-death-key-accused-still-large (accessed 22 November 2019).

17. https://timesofindia.indiatimes.com/city/mangaluru/abdul-basheer-succumbs-to-his-injuries-at-hospital/articleshow/62401601.cms.

18. The Karwan is a group of volunteers—writers, journalists, lawyers, teachers and researchers—who covered the length and breadth of this country visiting those ravaged by hate. It is not meant to be a research or fact-finding endeavour though it has ended up doing both. The author is part of Karwan. This write-up is based on the author's Karwan diaries.

19. As told to the Karwan team, this author included, in village Bhorahan, Sitamarhi, Bihar, on 25 February 2019.

20. As told to the Karwan team in Araria, Bihar, 27 February 2019.

21. Ibid.

22. As told to the Karwan team in village Hussainpur, Nuh, Haryana, 15 September 2017.

23. As told to the Karwan team in village Bhondsi, Haryana, 27 March 2019.

24. Ibid.

25. As told to the Karwan team by a group of farmers outside Pehlu Khan's house in village Jaisinghpur, Nuh, on 30 March 2018.

26. As told to the Karwan team in village Uttawarh, Palwal, 14 September 2017.

27. Ibid.

28. As told to the Karwan team by a group of farmers in village Bhango, district Nuh, 14 September 2017.

29. Ibid.

30. As told to the Karwan team by Qasim's wife, in Pilkhuwa, Hapur, Uttar Pradesh, 25 June 2018.

31. https://www.nationalheraldindia.com/india/bjp-goons-killed-qasim-qureshi-in-pilkhuwa-says-brother-at-delhi-protest-mob-lynching-hapur-uttar-pradesh.

32. As told to the Karwan team by women in the Muslim family who were victims of a mob attack in Bhondsi, Haryana, 27 March 2019.

33. As told to the Karwan team by the family of the slain man in Mangalore on 30 June 2018.

34. That the intent of the notification was not to prevent cruelty to animals but to harass people involved in the meat trade—Muslims and Dalits—was very clear. Section 22 of the rules, for instance, said: 'No person shall bring a cattle to an animal market unless upon arrival, he has furnished a written declaration signed by the owner or his authorized agent where details of the name, address, photo identity of the owner with details of identification of the cattle would be stated.' The declaration would also have to state that 'the cattle has not been brought for slaughter'. In situations where the animal has already been sold and brought to the market, the Animal Market Committee (AMC) would secure an undertaking that the animals were bought for agricultural purposes and not for slaughter. The AMC would keep a record of the name and address of the purchaser, verify that 'the person is an agriculturist by seeing the relevant revenue document', and shall secure a declaration from the purchaser that 'he shall not sell the animal up to six months from the date of purchase and abide by the rules'. Five copies of the proof of sale of an animal prior to its removal from the animal market have to be provided, with one copy each to the buyer, the seller, the tehsil office of the purchaser, the veterinary officer and the AMC.

35. Following widespread protests, the Centre initiated moves to withdraw its 23 May notification and was forced to scrap the controversial rules within a year. However, amid the mixed and contradictory messaging on the notification and its future, the gau rakshaks continued to ensure that transporting cattle is either very difficult or impossible.

36. The Gau Seva Aayog was established vide Haryana government notification no. S.O.13/HA.19\2010/S.3 and 4/2013 dated 25 January 2013.

37. https://hargauseva.gov.in/wp-content/uploads/2019/10/Standard-Term-and-Conditon-date.-03-06-2019.pdf.

38. https://www.dainiktribuneonline.com/2011/01. Bhani Ram Mangla was one of the chief organizers of the launch of the Gau Vansh Vikas Parokshth.

39. The Haryana Gau Seva Aayog Act, 2015, did not have the provision for the post of CEO, but the government amended the act to create the post. See 'IG to Be CEO of Gau Seva Aayog', *Tribune*, 2 February 2018, https://www.tribuneindia.com/news/haryana/ig-to-be-ceo-of-gau-seva-aayog/537335.html.

40. Akhlaque's violent death in Dadri found justification in the RSS mouthpiece *Panchjanya*. An article titled 'Is Utpaat Ke Us Paar' (The Other Side of This Mischief) states, 'Veda ka adesh hai ki gau hatya karne wale pataki ke pran le lo. Hum mein se bahuton ke liye to yah jivan–maran ka prashn hai' (Vedas order killing of the sinner who kills a cow. It is a matter of life and death for many of us); see https://www.indiatoday.in/india/story/vedas-order-killing-of-sinners-rss-mouthpiece-panchjanya-over-dadri-lynching-268656-2015-10-18; Union minister Jayant Sinha garlanded eight men convicted of lynching in Ramgarh, Jharkhand at his residence; see 'Union Minister Jayant Sinha Garlands 8 Lynching Convicts, Faces Opposition Flak', *Times of India*, 8 July 2018, https://timesofindia.indiatimes.com/india/union-minister-jayant-sinha-garlands-8-lynching-convicts-faces-opposition-flak/articleshow/64901863.cms. Shambhulal Regar, the man who lynched a Bengali migrant worker, Mohd Afrazul, who was working in Rajasthan's Rajsamand, was offered the ticket for contesting the Agra Lok Sabha seat by a Hindu political outfit, Navnirman Sena; see Uday Singh Rana, 'Shambhulal Regar, Who Hacked Muslim Man on Camera, May Contest Lok Sabha Polls From Agra', News18, 17 September 2018, https://www.news18.com/news/india/shambhulal-regar-who-hacked-

muslim-man-on-camera-may-contest-lok-sabha-polls-from-agra-1880263.html.

41. The election speech in Wardha, Maharashtra, 2 April 2019.

42. A. Bhattacharya, 'The "Secular" Forces Have Abandoned Secularism', Wire, 2019, https://thewire.in/politics/congress-bjp-secularism (accessed 22 November 2019).

43. Distressed by the increasing incidents of cow vigilantism in the country, three individuals—Martin Macwan, a Dalit rights activist, Mohanbhai Hamir Bhai Bedva, an alleged victim of such violence, and Tehseen Poonawalla, an activist lawyer—filed writ petitions in the Supreme Court in August 2016. They sought the Court to issue a directive to the Centre and some states to take action against cow vigilantes. The petitioners drew the Court's attention to the rise of incidents of cow vigilantism, where private citizens violently punish people who they suspect of consuming beef. The petitioners challenged the provisions of cow protection laws of six states protecting cow vigilantes—Rajasthan, Uttar Pradesh, Maharashtra, Gujarat, Jharkhand, and Karnataka. In particular, they challenged the provisions that prohibit any legal action against persons for actions done in 'good faith' under the law. Refer https://main.sci.gov.in/supremecourt/2016/27263/27263_2016_Judgement_17-Jul-2018.pdf.

44. Ahmar Afaq and Paras Nath Singh, 'One Year since the SC's Judgment, Lynchings Continue to "Corrode the Nation"', Leaflet, 17 July 2019, http://theleaflet.in/one-year-since-the-scs-judgment-lynchings-continue-to-corrode-the-nation.

45. https://www.indiatoday.in/india/story/committee-mob-violence-lynching-rajiv-gauba-1326666-2018-08-29.

46. Rameshwar Dayal v. State of Haryana, https://indiankanoon.org/doc/175568698.

47. Kabir Goswami, 'A Timeline: Six Accused Given Clean Chit In Pehlu Khan Lynching Case', News18, 14 September 2017, https://www.news18.com/news/india/a-timeline-six-accused-given-clean-chit-in-pehlu-khan-lynching-case-1518193.html.

48. In a bizarre move, the government of Maharashtra, in its policy on compensation for lynchings, added human trafficking as a category eligible for compensation equal to that of mob lynching. See Sharad Vyas, 'Victims of Mob Lynching, Human Trafficking in Maharashtra to Get Compensation', *The Hindu*, 9 May 2019, https://www.thehindu.com/news/national/other-states/victims-of-mob-lynching-human-trafficking-in-maharashtra-to-get-compensation/article27073792.ece.

49. Dhananjay Mahapatra, 'Supreme Court Seeks Response of Governments on Lynchings', *Times of India*, 27 July 2019, https://timesofindia.indiatimes.com/india/supreme-court-seeks-response-of-governments-on-lynchings/articleshow/70403754.cms.

50. While the prime minister has on occasion criticized the so-called gau rakshaks, the message has perhaps not been strong enough. For, a day after Rakbar Khan was lynched by a mob in Alwar in Rajasthan, BJP MLA Raja Singh said lynchings would continue until cow slaughter was banned in the country. In Uttar Pradesh, after a police inspector was killed by a rampaging mob, a BJP MLA argued that the policeman had shot himself and the mob had no role to play. See 'Human Rights Watch: Vigilante "Cow Protection" Groups Attack Minorities in India', IDSN, 19 February 2019, https://idsn.org/human-rights-watch-vigilante-cow-protection-groups-attack-minorities-in-india. BJP minister Jayant Sinha admitted in an interview that six people who were arrested in 2017 for lynching Alimuddin Ansari in Ramgarh were provided financial assistance by the BJP. See 'Year after Garlanding Jharkhand Lynching Accused, Jayant Sinha Reveals BJP Paid Their Legal Fees', News18, 3 May 2019, https://www.news18.com/news/india/year-after-garlanding-jharkhand-lynching-accused-jayant-sinha-reveals-bjp-paid-their-legal-fees-2127471.html.

51. On 26 July 2019, the Supreme Court issued notice to the Union home ministry, National Human Rights Commission of India (NHRC) and the state governments of Andhra Pradesh, Assam, Bihar, Gujarat, Jammu and Kashmir, Jharkhand, Madhya Pradesh, the National Capital Territory of Delhi (NCT), Rajasthan,

Uttar Pradesh and West Bengal, on a PIL petition alleging non-compliance with the Court's directions of 17 July 2018 for preventing cases of mob lynching.

Towards a New Equality Regime in India

1. Parts of this article were earlier published in 'Beyond Quotas and Commissions', *Seminar* 617 (2011).
2. The minority communities in India include Muslims, Sikhs, Christians, Buddhists and Zoroastrians (Parsis) notified as minority communities under Section 2(c) of the National Commission for Minorities Act, 1992. A gazette notification of 27 January 2014, further notified Jains as a minority community.
3. This discussion does not include other national commissions such as the National Human Rights Commission of India (NHRC) and Election Commission in that they are not mandated to look after interests of specific 'groups' of citizens.
4. The Ministry of Social Justice and Empowerment controls the National Commission for Scheduled Castes (NCSC) (established under Article 338 of the Constitution), National Commission for Backward Classes (NCBC), National Commission for Safai Karamcharis, National Commission for Denotified, Nomadic, and Semi-Nomadic Tribes (established in 2005), and also houses the Office of the Chief Commissioner for Persons with Disabilities, under the Persons with Disabilities (Equal Opportunities, Protection of Rights and Full Participation) Act, 1995. The Ministry of Tribal Affairs controls the National Commission for Scheduled Tribes (NCST) (under Article 338-A). NCST and NCSC were one until 2003 when a constitutional amendment created them into two separate entities. The Ministry of Women and Child Development is the proud helms(wo)man of two commissions—the National Commission for Women (NCW), and the National Commission for Protection of Child Rights (set up in March 2007 under the Commission for Protection of Child Rights Act of Parliament in December 2005). The Ministry of Minority Affairs, established

in 2006, took over the National Commission for Minorities (NCM), which was earlier located in the Ministry of Social Justice and Empowerment.

5. *Social, Economic and Educational Status of the Muslim Community of India: A Report* (Sachar Committee Report) (New Delhi: Government of India, 2006), p. 240.

6. The expert group headed by Prof. Madhava Menon came out with a report on the EOC, including a proposed bill.

7. Address by President Pratibha Patil to Parliament, New Delhi, 4 June 2009, http://pratibhapatil.nic.in/sp040609.html.

8. Article 15 (1): The State shall not discriminate against any citizen on grounds only of religion, race, caste, sex, place of birth or any of them. Article 16 (1): There shall be equality of opportunity for all citizens in matters relating to employment or appointment to any office under the State.

9. Annual Report, 2017–18, Delhi: National Commission for Women, 2018, p. 4.

10. http://ncw.nic.in/ncw-cells/complaint-investigation-cell (accessed 24 November 2019).

11. *India Today*, 'NCM Received 1498 Complaints in 2018', 7 April 2018, https://www.indiatoday.in/pti-feed/story/ncm-received-1498-complaints-in-2017-18-lowest-since-nda-came-to-power-in-centre-1206878-2018-04-07 (accessed 23 November 2019).

12. Farah Naqvi, 'An Unequal Opportunity Commission', *The Hindu*, 27 August 2010, https://www.thehindu.com/opinion/lead/An-Unequal-Opportunity-Commission/article16147138.ece.

13. https://timesofindia.indiatimes.com/india/Opportunities-panel-limited-to-minorities/articleshow/6301565.cms; https://economictimes.indiatimes.com/news/politics-and-nation/equal-opportunity-panel-for-minorities-soon/articleshow/6303216.cms.

Minorities, Market and Accumulation

1. This is a condensed and updated version of chapter three of *India's Market Society: Three Essays in Political Economy* (New Delhi: Three Essays Collective, 2005).

2. 2011 Census data, Government of India.

3. Raphael Susewind, 'Muslims in Indian Cities: Degrees of Segregation and the Elusive Ghetto', *Environment and Planning* 49, no. 6 (2017): 1286–1307.

4. See the Sachar Committee Report, especially chapter eight— *Social, Economic and Educational Status of the Muslim Community in India: A Report* (New Delhi: Government of India, 2006).

5. *Employment and Unemployment Situation Among Major Religious Groups in India: NSS 66th Round* (New Delhi: Government of India, 2013), Table 3.14R, p. 34.

6. S.R. Mondal, *Muslims of Siliguri* (New Delhi: Institute of Objective Studies/Qasi Publishing, 1997), p. 53.

7. Ibid.

8. Ibid.

9. I. Ahmad, 'Economic and Social Change', in *Muslims in India*, ed. Z. Imam (New Delhi: Orient Longman, 1975), pp. 246–47.

10. *Violent Cow Protection in India* (New York: Human Rights Watch, 2019), pp. 56–65, https://www.hrw.org/sites/default/files/report_pdf/india0219_web3.pdf.

11. Nilesh Jain, 'With Rising Cow Vigilantism, India's Leather Industry Takes a Hit', Quint, 31 August 2018, https://www.thequint.com/news/india/india-leather-industry-cow-vigilantism; Virendra Singh Rawat, 'Kumbh Effect: Beleaguered Kanpur Leather Industry Start Shifting to Kolkata', *Business Standard*, 5 April 2019, https://www.business-standard.com/article/companies/kumbh-effect-beleaguered-kanpur-leather-industry-start-shifting-to-kolkata-119040200247_1.html.

12. Mondal, *Muslims of Siliguri*, chapter five.

13. Omar Khalidi, *Indian Muslims since Independence* (New Delhi: Vikas Publishing House, 1995), pp. 70–73; Philippe Cadène, 'Network Specialists, Industrial Clusters and the Integration of Space in India', in *Decentralised Production in India: Industrial Districts, Flexible Specialisation and Employment,* ed. Philippe Cadène and Mark Holmstrom (New Delhi: SAGE, 1998), pp.139–168.

14. Ausaf Ahmad, *Indian Muslims: Issues in Social and Economic Development* (New Delhi: Khama Publishers, 1993), p. 41.

15. Khalidi, *Indian Muslims Since Independence*, p. 68.

16. T.P. Jr Wright, 'The New Muslim Businessmen of India: A Prospectus for Research' (paper presented at the Seventh European Conference on Modern South Asian Studies, School of Oriental and African Studies, University of London, 1981), p. 37.

17. Mattison Mines, *Muslim Merchants: The Economic Behaviour of an Indian Muslim Community* (New Delhi: Shri Ram Centre for Industrial Relations and Human Resources, 1972).

18. Ibid., pp. 93–98.

19. Ibid., p. 109 and pp. 112–18.

20. 2011 Census data.

21. John C.B. Webster, *The Dalit Christians: A History* (New Delhi: Indian Society for Promoting Christian Knowledge, 1992), p. 34.

22. V. Mathew Kurian, *The Caste-Class Formations: A Case Study of Kerala* (New Delhi: B.R. Publishing Corporation, 1986).

23. Paul D. Wiebe, *Christians in Andhra Pradesh: The Mennonites of Mahbubnagar* (Madras: The Christian Literature Society, 1988), p. 192.

24. Webster, *The Dalit Christians*, p. 10.

25. David Mosse, 'Idioms of Subordination and Styles of Protest among Christian and Hindu Harijan Castes in Tamil Nadu', *Contributions to Indian Sociology* 28.1 (1994), pp. 67–106; see also Mosse, 'Caste and Development: Contemporary Perspectives on a Structure of Discrimination and Advantage', *World Development* 110 (2018): 422–36.

26. Mosse, 'Idioms of Subordination and Styles of Protest among Christian and Hindu Harijan castes in Tamil Nadu', pp. 67–106.

27. Ibid, p. 82.

28. Ibid.

29. Godwin Shiri, *The Plight of Christian Dalits: A South Indian Case Study* (Bangalore: Asian Trading Corporation, 1997), pp. 115–34, 242.

30. https://www.hrw.org/reports/1999/indiachr/christians8-03.htm.

31. See reports in *Communalism Watch and Governance Monitor*, http://www.saccer.org. Monthly reports of attacks on people and property also reveal the emergence of a new social movement of

poor Christians consisting of a set of organizations with economic agendas.
32. 2011 Census data.
33. Paul Wallace, 'The Sikhs as a "Minority" in a Sikh Majority State in India', *Asian Survey* 26.3 (1986): 363–377. This concentration is now less marked.
34. Arvinder Singh, 'Industrial Transition in an Agricultural Surplus Region: A Study of Punjab' (PhD diss., Jawaharlal Nehru University, 1999), p. 191.
35. Ibid.
36. 2011 Census data.
37. P.N. Chopra, ed., *Religions and Communities of India* (New Delhi: Vision Books, 1998), p. 167.
38. James Laidlaw, *Riches and Renunciation: Religion, Economy, and Society among the Jains* (Oxford: Clarendon Press, 1996), p. 87.
39. Ibid, pp. 349–50.
40. Ibid, pp. 354–55.
41. Ibid, pp. 355–56.
42. Christine M. Cottam Ellis, 'The Jain Merchant Castes of Rajasthan: Some Aspects of the Management of Social Identity in a Market Town', in *The Assembly of Listeners: Jains in Society*, edited by Michael Carrithers and Caroline Humphrey (Cambridge: Cambridge University Press, 1991), pp. 75–107.
43. 2011 Census data.
44. T.M. Luhrmann, 'The Good Parsi: The Postcolonial "Feminization" of a Colonial Elite', *Man* 29.2 (1994): 333–57; P. Axelrod, 'Cultural and Historical Factors in the Population Decline of the Parsis of India', *Population Studies* 44.3 (1990): 401–19.
45. Amalendu Guha, 'More about the Parsi Seths—Their Roots, Entrepeneurship and Comprador Role, 1650–1918', *Economic and Political Weekly* 19.3: 117–32; Luhrmann, 'The Good Parsi: The Postcolonial "Feminization" of a Colonial Elite'.
46. Werner Sombart, *The Jews and Modern Capitalism* (Glencoe, Illinois: Free Press, 1951), p. 274.
47. Barbara Harriss-White, *India Working: Essays on Society and Economy* (Cambridge: Cambridge University Press, 2002); Harriss-White,

ed., *Middle India and Urban-Rural Development: Four Decades of Change* (New Delhi: Springer, 2016).

48. K.M. Panikkar, *The Foundations of New India* (London: George Allen and Unwin, 1963), p. 33.

The Triple Talaq Controversy: A Sociolegal View

1. *Shayara Bano v. Union of India and Others*, https://sci.gov.in/supremecourt/2016/6716/6716_2016_Judgement_22-Aug-2017.pdf.

2. *Shamim Ara v. State of Uttar Pradesh*, https://sci.gov.in/jonew/judis/18797.pdf.

3. Commenting on the judgment, Islamic scholar Tahir Mahmood lamented, 'How I wish the bench had just reiterated Shamim Ara, unanimously, approving this implication of the very sensible ruling given 15 years ago.' Tahir Mahmood, 'All's Well that Ends Well', *Indian Express*, 23 August 2017, https://indianexpress.com/article/opinion/columns/alls-well-that-ends-well-triple-talaq-4809006.

4. As per Article 141 of the Constitution, the Supreme Court verdict is the law of the land.

5. Press Trust of India, 'No Need for New Law on Triple Talaq; SC Verdict Law of the Land: Government', *Times of India*, 22 August 2017, https://timesofindia.indiatimes.com/india/no-need-for-new-law-on-triple-*Talaq*-sc-verdict-law-of-the-land-government/articleshow/60179929.cms.

6. Faizan Mustafa, 'Why Criminalising Triple Talaq is Unnecessary Overkill', Wire, 15 December 2017, https://thewire.in/gender/why-criminalising-triple-*Talaq*-is-unnecessary-overkill.

7. PTI, 'Bill to Ban Triple Talaq to Be Brought Again: Ravi Shankar Prasad', *Economic Times*, 3 June 2019, https://economictimes.indiatimes.com/news/politics-and-nation/bill-to-ban-triple-*talaq*-to-be-brought-again-ravi-shankar-prasad/articleshow/69632691.cms?from=mdr.

8. 'President Ram Nath Kovind gives assent to triple talaq Bill', *The Hindu*, 1 August 2019, https://www.thehindu.com/news/

national/president-ram-nath-kovind-gives-assent-to-triple-*talaq*-bill/article28780061.ece.

9. Gopika Solanki, *Adjudication in Religious Family Law: Cultural Accommodation, Legal Pluralism, and Gender Equality in India* (New Delhi: Cambridge University Press, 2011); Sylvia Vatuk, *Marriage and Its Discontents: Women, Islam and the Law in India* (New Delhi: Women Unlimited, 2017).

10. Anindita Chakrabarti and Suchandra Ghosh, 'Judicial Reform vs Adjudication of Personal Law', *Economic and Political Weekly* 52.49 (2017): 12–14.

11. Justice Dave was a judge of the Gujarat High Court when Prime Minister Modi was the chief minister of the state. In August 2014, while speaking at a conference at Gujarat University, he made the following comment, 'Had I been the dictator of India, I would have introduced Gita and Mahabharata in Class I,' which was immediately picked up by the media. See 'If I Were Dictator, Would Have Made Gita Compulsory in Class I: SC Judge', *Indian Express*, 3 August 2014, http://indianexpress.com/article/india/india-others/if-i-were-dictator-would-have-made-gita-compulsory-in-class-i-sc-judge.

12. Refer https://sci.gov.in/jonew/judis/43087.pdf

13. *Re: Muslim Women's Quest for Equality v. Jamiat Ulma-I-Hind*, suo motu writ petition (civil) no. 2 of 2015.

14. Tahir Mahmood, 'Ball in the Supreme Court', *Indian Express*, 15 May 2017, http://indianexpress.com/article/opinion/columns/ball-in-the-supreme-court-triple-*Talaq*-4655854/.

15. It needs to be clarified that several Shia sects such as Khojas, Bohras, Ismailis, Ithna Asharis do not recognize instant triple talaq and have provided elaborate dispute resolution mechanisms for arbitration in family matters. Even among Sunnis there are sects such as Ahl-e-Hadeez who do not recognize instant triple talaq. However, a majority of north Indian Muslims are Hanafis who recognize instant triple talaq. Instant triple talaq is not the only form available to a Muslim couple to dissolve their marriage. The Muslim law recognizes several other forms including the woman's right to dissolve the marriage—khula,

divorce by mutual consent—mubarra, and a divorce pronounced by a qazi—fasq.

16. AIMPLB is a representative body of Muslims of various denominations. However, it is dominated by clerics of the Hanafi sect. Though it is a non-statutory body, it has a great influence over matters of faith among followers of the Sunni sect of Islam in India.

17. Abusaleh Shariff and Syed Khalid, 'Abandoned Women Vastly Outnumber Victims of Triple Talaq and It's Time Modi Spoke Up for Them', Wire, 17 April 2017, https://thewire.in/gender/abandoned-women-triple-talaq.

18. *India Today*, 'Yogi Adityanath Compares Triple Talaq to Draupadi's Cheer-haran, Calls for Common Civil Code', 17 April 2017, https://www.indiatoday.in/india/story/yogi-adityanath-triple-talaq-draupadi-cheer-haran-common-civil-code-971856-2017-04-17.

19. News18, 'UP Minister Says Muslims Use Triple Talaq to Change Wives, Satisfy "Lust"', 29 April 2017, http://www.news18.com/news/politics/up-minister-says-muslims-use-triple-*Talaq*-to-change-wives-satisfy-lust-1387283.html.

20. *State of Bombay v. Narasu Appa Mali*, in *All India Reporter*, 1952, Bombay, p. 84.

21. In the talaq-e-ahasan mode, a single pronouncement of talaq is made during the time of menstrual purity (tuhr) followed by an iddat period of three lunar months (ninety days), and if the wife is pregnant, until her delivery. In the talaq-e-hasan mode, the husband pronounces talaq every month, during the three months of the iddat period when the wife is in a state of menstrual purity. In both forms, the husband must abstain from cohabitation. In the event of cohabitation, the talaq is automatically revoked. The husband must provide shelter and maintenance to the wife in the matrimonial home during the iddat period. The marriage is dissolved upon the expiry of the iddat period only if no cohabitation has taken place during the period of iddat. The iddat period is supposed to be a cooling period, during which the

couple can reunite. See Asaf A.A. Fyzee, *Outlines of Muhammadan Law* (New Delhi: Oxford University Press, 2002), pp.152–54.

22. Dhananjay Mahapatra, 'Supreme Court Leaves Uniform Civil Code to Parliament, Door Ajar on Triple Talaq', *Times of India*, 8 December 2015, http://timesofindia.indiatimes.com/india/ Supreme-Court-leaves-uniform-civil-code-to-Parliament-door-ajar-on-triple-*Talaq*/articleshow/50083462.cms.

23. Shalini Nair, 'Shayara Banu's fight against triple talaq', *Indian Express*, 24 April 2016, http://indianexpress.com/article/india/ india-news-india/triple-*Talaq*-supreme-court-ban-muslim-india-shayara-banu-2767412.

24. *Danial Latifi v. Union of India,* https://sci.gov.in/jonew/ judis/18025.pdf.

25. 2003 (1) BomCR 740.

26. 1981 (1) GLR 358.

27. 1981 (1) GLR 375.

28. *Parveen Akhtar v. Union of India*, 2003 (1) LW(Crl) 115; *Najmunbee v. S.K. Sikander S.K. Rehman*, I (2004) DMC 211; *Mustari Begum v. Mirza Mustaque Baig*, II (2005) DMC 94; *Shahzad v. Anisa Bee*, II (2006) DMC 229; *Farida Bano v. Kamruddin*, II (2006) DMC 698 MP; *Dilshad Begaum Pathan v. Ahmadkhan Hanifkhan Pathan*, II (2007) DMC 738; *Riaz Fatima v. Mohd. Sharif*, I (2007) DMC 26; *Shakil Ahmad Jalaluddin Shaikh v. Vahida Shakil Shaikh*, MANU/ MH/0501/2016.

29. Paula Thompson, Rhonda Itaoui and Dr Hatem Bazian, *Islamophobia in India: Stoking Bigotry* (Berkeley, California: Islamophobia Studies Centre, 2019).

30. Zakia Pathak and Rajeswari Sunder Rajan, 'Shahbano', *Signs* 14.3 (1989): 558–82.

31. Flavia Agnes, 'Women's Movement within a Secular Framework: Redefining the Agenda', *Economic and Political Weekly* 29.19 (1994): 1123–28.

32. Consultation Paper on 'Reform of Family Law', Law Commission of India, Government of India, 31 August 2018, http://www. lawcommissionofindia.nic.in/reports/CPonReformFamilyLaw.pdf

The Violence of Law

1. Maharashtra Control of Organized Crime (MCOC) Special Case no. 1 of 2009.

2. For a potted history of the various blasts during this period, see Vappala Balachandran, 'Will the NIA "Supplementary Chargesheet" End the Confusion on the Malegaon Blasts', Wire, 16 May 2016, https://thewire.in/politics/will-the-nia-supplementary-charge-sheet-end-the-confusion-on-malegaon-blasts.

3. Sunanda Mehta, 'Since This New Govt Came, I Have Been Told to Go Soft on Accused (Hindu extremists): Special Public Prosecutor Rohini Salian', Indian Express, 25 June 2015, https://indianexpress.com/article/india/india-others/since-this-new-govt-came-i-have-been-told-to-go-soft-on-accused-hindu-extremists-special-public-prosecutor.

4. PTI, 'BJP Uses Samjhauta Blast Verdict to Slam Congress', Economic Times, 29 March 2019, https://economictimes.indiatimes.com/news/elections/lok-sabha/india/bjp-uses-samjhauta-blast-verdict-to-slam-congress/articleshow/68628960.cms; also see News18, 'Mecca Masjid Blast Case: BJP Says Politics of 'Defaming' Hindus Exposed, Congress Questions NIA', 16 April 2018, https://www.news18.com/news/politics/mecca-masjid-blast-case-bjp-says-politics-of-defaming-hindus-exposed-congress-questions-nia-1720271.html.

5. Mohammed Iqbal, 'Shinde Blasts BJP, RSS for "Inciting Hindu terror"', The Hindu, 20 January 2013, https://www.thehindu.com/news/national/shinde-blasts-bjp-rss-for-inciting-hindu-terror/article4325767.ece.

6. PTI, 'Hindu Terror Is a Misnomer, Says RSS Chief', Rediff, 17 October 2010, https://www.rediff.com/news/report/hindu-terror-is-amisnomer-says-rss-chief/20101017.htm.

7. NDTV, 'We The People—Right-wing Terror: a Serious Threat?', http://www.ndtv.com/video/player/we-the-people/right-wing-terrorism-real-threat-or-overstated/265259?video-mostpopularEx-cop.

8. Ibid.

9. Anil Kalhan, et al., 'Colonial Continuities: Human Rights, Terrorism, and Security Laws in India', *Columbia Journal of Asian Law* 20.1 (2006): 147. See Chapter IV: 'Contemporary Antiterrorism Laws': 141–172.

10. Rohit Prajapati, 'Anti-terror Laws: Tools of State Terror' (submission to South Asia sub-regional hearing, International Commission of Jurists, New Delhi, 27–28 February 2007).

11. *Lawless Roads: A Report on TADA, 1985-1993* (Delhi: People's Union for Democratic Rights, 1993).

12. In a case of dispute over a water chestnut pond in Bhadasi (Arwal) dating to 1988, in which a police officer and three alleged 'extremists' lost their lives, twenty persons belonging to the poorest sections of society faced trial for the alleged commission of various offences punishable under the Indian Penal Code (IPC), TADA Act and Arms Act. The accused were given life imprisonment (two died during trial and two were held to be juveniles) by the Sessions Judge, Jahanabad-cum-Special Judge, TADA. See *Madan Singh v. State of Bihar,* https://main.sci.gov.in/jonew/judis/26032.pdf. Similarly, the Bhadasi killings of Bhumihar landlords by low-caste landless labourers in 1992 in Gaya was tried and prosecuted under TADA. Death sentences were also handed out in this case but appeals in the Supreme Court ended either in commutation or acquittal. See *Krishna Mochi v. State of Bihar,* https://main.sci.gov.in/jonew/judis/18388.pdf; *Bihari Manjhi and Others v. State of Bihar,* https://main.sci.gov.in/jonew/judis/18391.pdf; 'Rajendra Paswan versus State of Bihar', 2002 (4) SCC 352; 'Vyas Ram @ Vyas Kahar and Others versus State of Bihar', https://main.sci.gov.in/jonew/judis/40818.pdf.

13. 'Citizens Speak Out against TADA, POTA and AFSPA', *Liberation*, 6 August 2004, http://archive.cpiml.org/liberation/year_2004/september/TADA_NewDelhi.htm.

14. National Human Rights Commission, New Delhi, India. Annual Report 1994–95. https://www.rwi.lu.se/NHRIDB/Asia/India/Annual%20Report%2094-95.pdf.

15. Manoj Mitta, *The Fiction of Fact-Finding: Modi and Godhra* (New Delhi: HarperCollins, 2014).

16. Manisha Sethi, *Kafkaland: Prejudice, Law and Counterterrorism in India* (Gurgaon: Three Essays Collective, 2014), p. 27. Also see Sethi, 'An Architect of Conscience: Mukul Sinha (1951–2014)', *Economic and Political Weekly* 49.22 (31 May 2014), http://www.epw.in/journal/2014/22/web-exclusives/architect-conscience.html.
17. Kalhan et al., 'Colonial Continuities': 180.
18. Ibid, 181.
19. Bail order of the Bombay High Court in criminal bail applications 1536, 1634 and 1692 of 2012, 31 January 2013.
20. Special Public Prosecutor's arguments; see Ibid,14.
21. *State of Kerala v. Raneef,* https://main.sci.gov.in/jonew/judis/37314.pdf.
22. Mayur Suresh, 'The Slow Erosion of Fundamental Rights: How *Romila Thapar v. Union of India* Highlights What Is Wrong with the UAPA', *Indian Law Review* 3.2 (2019): 212–23.
23. Mayur Suresh and Jawahar Raja, *Detrimental to the Peace, Integrity and Secular Fabric of India: The Case against the Students' Islamic Movement of India* (New Delhi: Jawaharlal Nehru University, 2012), p. 10.
24. *Guilt by Association: UAPA Cases from Madhya Pradesh* (New Delhi: Jamia Teachers' Solidarity Association, 2013).
25. Translation: 'Even if a wave of blood were to pass over my head/ It is not as if I would get up from the beloved's doors.'
26. FIR no. 3036/2008, 1 April 2008 at PS Vijaypur Naka, Solapur City, Maharashtra.
27. IANS, 'Malegaon 2006 Blasts: Court Discharges All Eight Muslim Accused', *Business Standard*, 25 April 2016, https://www.business-standard.com/article/current-affairs/malegaon-2006-blasts-court-discharges-all-eight-muslim-accused-116042500688_1.html.
28. Chaitanya Mallapur and Devyani Chhetri, 'Why Arrested Activists Shouldn't Despair: 67% Unlawful Activities Prevention Act Cases Ended In Acquittal/Discharge', IndiaSpend, 8 September 2018, http://www.indiaspend.com/cover-story/why-arrested-activists-shouldnt-despair-67-unlawful-activities-prevention-act-cases-ended-in-acquittaldischarge-99067.
29. *Guilt by Association*, p. 14.

30. *Jamaat-E-Islami Hind vs Union of India*, 1995 SCC (1) 428, JT 1995 (1) 31.
31. Ibid, see paras 21 and 26.
32. See discussion on this aspect in Suresh and Raja, *Detrimental to the Peace, Integrity and Secular Fabric of India*, op. cit., pp. 14–15.
33. Award dated 4 August 2010 of Unlawful Activities (Prevention) Act Tribunal presided over by Justice Sanjeev Khanna at paras 320-321.
34. Ibid, p. 10.
35. Affidavit of B.P.S. Parihar (PW 58) before the Unlawful Activities (Prevention) Tribunal, New Delhi, in the matter of Students' Islamic Movement of India, Notification no. 260 (e) dated 5 February 2010. Copy on record.
36. PTI, 'News of SIMI Encounter to Enhance Morale of Nation: Jitendra Singh', *Indian Express*, 3 November 2016, https:// indianexpress.com/article/india/india-news-india/news-of-simi-encounter-to-enhance-morale-of-nation-jitendra-singh-3731310.
37. NDTV, 'Terror Suspects Fed "Chicken Biryani": Chief Minister Chouhan On SIMI Row', 2 November 2016, https://www.ndtv.com/india-news/after-simi-shooting-chief-minister-chouhan-talks-of-biryani-in-jail-1620410.
38. Lok Sabha Proceedings, Fourteenth Series, Vol. XXXVI, Wednesday, 17 December 2008. Accessible at: http://164.100.47.194/debatestext/14/17-12-2008.pdf.
39. PTI, 'Controversial Gujarat Anti-terror Law Gets President Assent on 4th Attempt', *India Today*, 5 November 2019, https://www.indiatoday.in/india/story/gujarat-anti-terror-law-president-assent-4th-attempt-1615934-2019-11-05.
40. PTI, 'Will Make Sedition Law More Stringent, Says Rajnath Singh', *India Today*, 15 May 2019, https://www.indiatoday.in/elections/lok-sabha-2019/story/will-make-sedition-law-more-stringent-says-rajnath-singh-1525890-2019-05-15.
41. The Unlawful Activities (Prevention) Amendment Act, 2019 (No. 28 of 2019). *Gazette of India* notification, 8 August 2019.
42. The NIA exonerated Pragya in a supplementary report u/s. 173(8) of the Code of Criminal Procedure it filed on 13 May 2015. In

court of Special Judge under MCOCA, 1999, and NIA Act, 2008, for Greater Mumbai at Mumbai.

The Crisis of Citizenship and the 'Bangladeshi' Paradox

1. Dr B.R. Ambedkar, *Constituent Assembly Debates, Volume IX* (Delhi: Lok Sabha Secretariat, 2003), p. 347.
2. Dr Rajendra Prasad, *Constituent Assembly Debates, Volume IX*, p. 343.
3. Jawaharlal Nehru, *Constituent Assembly Debates, Volume IX*, p. 399.
4. Pandit Thakur Das Bhargava, *Constituent Assembly Debates, Volume IX*, p. 382.
5. *The Hindu*, 'Infiltrators Are Termites, Will Throw Them Out: Amit Shah', 11 April 2019, https://www.thehindu.com/elections/lok-sabha-2019/infiltrators-are-termites-will-throw-them-out-amit-shah/article26805646.ece (accessed 22 November 2019).
6. Monirul Hussain, *The Assam Movement: A Sociological Study*, Phd dissertation submitted to JNU (New Delhi, 1989), pp. 16–17.
7. The Hindutva discourse makes a separation between refugees and infiltrators. Hindus and other Indic communities are considered as victims of persecution, and declared legitimate refugees. The Muslim immigrant, on the other hand, is an infiltrator whose intentions are suspect.
8. S.K. Sinha, Report on the Illegal Migration into Assam (Submitted to President of India), Raj Bhavan Guwahati, D. O. No. GSAG.3/98/, Nov 8, 1998, para 24, chapter 2, https://www.satp.org/satporgtp/countries/india/states/assam/documents/papers/illegal_migration_in_assam.htm#CONTENTS
9. Justice R.F. Nariman, 'Assam Sanmilita Mahasangha and Others versus Union of India and Others', 20.3 and 20.4. Refer https://sci.gov.in/jonew/judis/42194.pdf.
10. Monirul Hussain, *The Assam Movement: Class, Ideology and Movement* (New Delhi: Manak Publications, 1994), pp. 134–35.
11. *Asam Bani*, 18 August 1994.
12. It is to note that during the same period when Assam exhibited a declining trend, the rest of the north-east region returned growth figures far above the national average.

13. While religious distribution of migration inflows and outflows can be measured using this indirect method, according to Barooah, there was virtually no way in which the legality of migrant status could be determined—whether they had legally entered Assam or illegally, whether they came from Bangladesh, Nepal or from any other part of the country—except on the basis of certain assumptions. These assumptions are: a. All Muslims who came to Assam between 1971 to 2001 were illegal Bangladeshis and continued to stay in the state. (By this estimate, there will be a maximum presence of 5,02,000 illegal Bangladeshis in the state in the year 2011.) b. All Muslim migrants who entered Assam were illegal Bangladeshis and all those who left the state were also the same. (This would leave a minimum number of 1,25,000 illegal Bangladeshis in Assam or 1.1 per cent of the state's Muslim population.) See Vani K. Barooah, 'The Killing Fields of Assam: The Myth and Reality of Its Muslim Immigration' (University of Ulster, 2012), pp. 7–8. Assessed online at MPRA, https://mpra.ub.uni-muenchen.de/75672.

14. The exactness of the NRC of 1951 is uncertain. It was prepared as a secret administrative document on the basis of 'census slips' by officials not professionally trained to do so. The enumeration was hurriedly completed within a period of twenty days, and given the enormity of the irregularities that had crept in, the entire project to prepare the NRC was abandoned by the registrar general of census operations. Later, the courts too refused to accept the NRC of 1951 as evidence of citizenship. See Binayak Dutta, 'The Unending Conundrum: The Story of Citizens/Foreigners between Politics and the Law in Assam', *Pangsau*, 31 May 2018, https://pangsau.com/2018/05/31/the-unending-conundrum-the-story-of-citizens-foreigners-between-politics-and-the-law-in-assam/.

15. While enforcing the act, numerous people were pushed into East Pakistan without any trial up to 1964. The arrested people were not provided with any opportunity to prove their citizenship. See Abdul Mannan, *Infiltration: Genesis of Assam Movement* (Guwahati: SAS Publishers, 2017), p. 33.

16. The provision was rarely followed and the border police continued to enjoy a free hand in arresting suspected illegal

residents. According to Mannan, until the 1970s quite a few lakh Bengal-origin Indian citizens were deported applying various tactics of labelling them as Pakistani citizens. See Mannan, *Infiltration*, pp. 33–34.

17. In February 2017, Assam's parliamentary affairs minister informed the House that a total of 4,44,189 people were referred to the tribunals. Nearly half of the cases remained pending with the tribunals. Of the cases resolved, 92 per cent were able to prove their citizenship, and of those declared foreigners, a majority were ex-parte judgments. See Abdul Kalam Azad, 'The Struggle of 'Doubtful Voters' Has Intensified in BJP's Assam', Wire, 12 July 2017, https://thewire.in/law/assam-doubtful-voters-sonowal.

Kashmiri Pandits: The Ambiguous Minority

1. Mridu Rai, *Hindu Rulers, Muslim Subjects: Islam, Rights, and the History of Kashmir* (London: Hurst & Co., 2004).
2. Ibid.
3. See Rai, *Hindu Rulers, Muslim Subjects*; Chitralekha Zutshi, *Languages of Belonging: Islam, Regional Identity, and the Making of Kashmir* (London: Hurst & Co., 2004).
4. Ashutosh Varshney, 'India, Pakistan, and Kashmir: Antinomies of Nationalism', *Asian Survey* 31.11 (1991): 997–1019.
5. Cabeiri deBergh Robinson, *Body of Victim, Body of Warrior: Refugee Families and the Making of Kashmiri Jihadists* (Berkeley: University of California Press, 2013).
6. Christopher Snedden. 'What Happened to Muslims in Jammu? Local Identity, '"the Massacre" of 1947' and the Roots of the 'Kashmir Problem', *South Asia: Journal of South Asian studies* 24.2 (2001): 111–34.
7. The matter of Article 370 is controversial. This article is often referred to by the Indian state, in both liberal and national forms, to deflect criticism of its policies towards Kashmir. Within the Indian mainstream, the repealing of Article 370 was often used in political rhetoric by parties such as the BJP. The recent abrogation

in August 2019 followed by the reorganization of Jammu and Kashmir from a state into two Union Territories by the BJP-led regime in New Delhi removes any legal and moral cover used by the Indian state in the past to present its relationship to Jammu and Kashmir as a fair one. It will be important to see what the future now holds. See A.G. Noorani, *Article 370: A Constitutional History of Jammu and Kashmir* (New Delhi: Oxford University Press, 2015).

8. Balraj Puri, *Kashmir: Towards Insurgency* (New Delhi: Orient Longman, 1995).

9. Sumantra Bose, *The Challenge in Kashmir: Democracy, Self-Determination, and a Just Peace* (New Delhi: SAGE, 1997).

10. Ananya Jahanara Kabir, *Territory of Desire: Representing the Valley of Kashmir* (Minneapolis: University of Minnesota Press, 2009).

11. Ibid.

12. Ankur Datta, *Culture Summary: Kashmiri* (New Haven: Human Relations Area Files, 2019) https://ehrafworldcultures.yale.edu/document?id=av04-000.

13. Alexander Evans, 'A Departure from History: Kashmiri Pandits 1990–2001', *Contemporary South Asia* 11.1 (2002): 19–37.

14. Triloki Nath Madan, *Family and Kinship: A Study of the Pandits of Rural Kashmir* (New Delhi: Oxford University Press, 2002).

15. See Anand Koul, *The Kashmiri Pandit* (New Delhi: Utpal Publications, 1991); Jia Lal Kilam, *A History of Kashmiri Pandits* (New Delhi: Utpal Publications, 2003); R.K. Parmu, *A History of Muslim Rule in Kashmir, 1320–1819* (New Delhi: People's Publishing House, 1969); P.N.K. Bamzai, *Kashmir & Central Asia* (New Delhi: Light and Life Publishers, 1980).

16. Kusum Pant, *The Kashmiri Pandit: Story of a Community in Exile* (New Delhi: Allied Publishers, 1987).

17. Henny Sender, *The Kashmiri Pandits: A Study of Cultural Choice in North India* (New Delhi: Oxford University Press, 1988).

18. Veena Das, *Critical Events: An Anthropological Perspective on Contemporary India* (New Delhi: Oxford University Press, 1995).

19. Triloki Nath Madan, 'Religious Ideology in a Plural Society: The Muslims and Hindus of Kashmir', *Contributions to Indian Sociology* (New Series) 6.1 (1972): 106–41.
20. Zutshi, *Languages of Belonging*.
21. Ankur Datta, *On Uncertain Ground: Displaced Kashmiri Pandits in Jammu and Kashmir* (New Delhi: Oxford University Press, 2017).
22. Sudha Koul, *The Tiger Ladies: A Memoir of Kashmir* (Boston: Beacon Press, 2002), p. 106.
23. Prem Nath Bazaz, *The History of Struggle for Freedom in Kashmir: Cultural and Politics, from the Earliest Times to the Present Day* (Srinagar: Kashmir Publishing Company, 1954).
24. Mushtaq A. Kaw, 'Land Rights in Rural Kashmir: A Study in Continuity and Change from Late-Sixteenth to Late-Twentieth Centuries', in *The Valley of Kashmir: The Making and Unmaking of a Composite Culture?*, ed. Aparna Rao (New Delhi: Manohar Books, 2008), pp. 207–34.
25. See C.J. Fuller and Haripriya Narasimhan, *Tamil Brahmans: The Making of a Middle-Class Caste* (Chicago: University of Chicago Press, 2014); Frank F. Conlon, *A Caste in a Changing World: The Chitrapur Saraswat Brahmans, 1700–1935* (New Delhi: Thompson Press, 1977).
26. Datta, *On Uncertain Ground*.
27. Ibid., p. 64.
28. Rahul Pandita, *Our Moon Has Blood Clots: The Exodus of the Kashmiri Pandits* (Noida: Random House India, 2013).
29. Siddhartha Gigoo, *The Garden of Solitude* (New Delhi: Rupa Publications, 2010).
30. Ankur Datta, 'Dealing with Dislocation: Migration, Place and Home among Displaced Kashmiri Pandits in Jammu and Kashmir', *Contributions to Indian Sociology* 50.1 (2016): 58.
31. Haley Duschinski, '"Survival Is Now Our Politics": Kashmiri Hindu Community Identity and the Politics of Homeland', *International Journal of Hindu Studies* 12.1 (2008): 41–64.
32. Datta, 'Dealing with dislocation: Migration, place and home among displaced Kashmiri Pandits in Jammu and Kashmir': 69.

Is There a Future for Urdu?

1. Ather Farouqui, 'The Problem of Urdu in India—Political or Existential? An Interview with S.R. Faruqi', *Annual of Urdu Studies* 10 (1995): 157.
2. Bernard Weinraub, 'Decline of Urdu Feared in India', *New York Times*, 5 August 1973, https://www.nytimes.com/1973/08/05/archives/decline-of-urdu-feared-in-india-14-recognized-languages.html.
3. Shams Ur Rehman Alavi, 'Census Data on Language Reveals a Surprise about Urdu', Wire, 6 July 2018, https://thewire.in/culture/urdu-census-language-2011-north-india.
4. M. Hamid Ansari, 'Urdu is dying a slow death', *Pioneer*, 9 February 2014, https://www.dailypioneer.com/2014/sunday-edition/urdu-is-dying-a-slow-death.html.
5. Samanwaya Rautray, 'Supreme Court approves Urdu as second official language of Uttar Pradesh', *Economic Times*, 5 September 2014, https://economictimes.indiatimes.com/news/politics-and-nation/supreme-court-approves-urdu-as-second-official-language-of-uttar-pradesh/articleshow/41708810.cms.
6. Ather Farouqui, 'Salvaging Urdu from Degradation', review of *The Oxford India Anthology of Modern Urdu Literature: Poetry and Prose Miscellany*, edited by Mehr Afshan Farooqi, *Economic and Political Weekly* 43.18 (May 2008): 27–28.
7. Abdul Shaban, *Urdu Medium Schools in Maharashtra: An Assessment of their Infrastructure and Possibility of Developing Them in Model Schools* (Mumbai: Tata Institute of Social Sciences, 2014), https://mdd.maharashtra.gov.in/Site/Upload/Pdf/Combined_Urdu_medium_Schools_report.pdf.
8. Hasan Abdullah, 'Urdu in India, its Present State, and the Way Forward', in *Redefining Urdu Politics in India*, ed. Ather Farouqui (New Delhi: Oxford University Press, 2006), pp. 219–20.
9. 'Hindi is losing its stature among millennial kids and parents are to blame too', *India Today*, 10 July 2019, https://www.indiatoday.in/education-today/featurephilia/story/hindi-is-losing-its-

stature-among-millennial-kids-and-parents-are-to-blame-too-1565828-2019-07-10.

10. G.N. Devy, *The Crisis Within: On Knowledge and Education in India* (New Delhi: Aleph Book Company, 2017), p. 15.

11. Ankita Pandey, 'Urdu newspapers: growing, not dying', *Hoot*, 4 October 2016, http://asu.thehoot.org/research/research-studies/urdu-newspapers-growing-not-dying-9683.

12. 'Only 12% Hindi Speakers Bilingual: Census', *Times of India*, 13 November 2018, https://timesofindia.indiatimes.com/india/indias-most-and-least-tongue-tied-communities/articleshow/66600187.cms.

13. Shaban, *Urdu Medium Schools in Maharashtra*.

Education and the Muslim Child

1. Azra Razzack, 'Growing Up Muslim', *Seminar* 387 (1991): 30–31.

2. *Social, Economic and Educational Status of the Muslim Community of India: A Report (Sachar Committee Report)* (New Delhi: Government of India, 2006).

3. See Mushirul Hasan, *Legacy of a Divided Nation: Indian Muslims since Independence* (New Delhi: OUP, 1997).

4. Ibid.

5. See Mushir ul Haq, *Islam in Secular India* (Indian Institute of Advanced Study, 1972).

6. M. Mujeeb, *The Indian Muslims* (New Delhi: Munshiram Manoharlal Publishers, 2003).

7. For a detailed analysis of the educational discourse, see Azra Razzack, *Education and the Emergence of Muslim Identity in India*, PhD thesis (University of Delhi, 1998).

8. *Report of the Education Commission, 1964–66* (New Delhi: Ministry of Education, 1966).

9. For a detailed analysis, see Razzack, *Education and the Emergence of Muslim Identity in India*, PhD thesis (University of Delhi: 1998). However, this analysis is based on texts being used by the National Council of Educational Research and Training before the turn of this century. The new textbooks introduced after the National

Curriculum Framework 2005 gave more space to diversity and are more inclusive.

10. Nazia Erum, *Mothering a Muslim: The Dark Secret in Our Schools and Playgrounds* (New Delhi: Juggernaut, 2017).

11. *Mushawarat* 3.13 (July–September, 2003): 42.

12. See a discussion in Tanya Matthan, Chandana Anusha and Meenakshi Thapan, 'Being Muslims, Becoming Citizens: A Muslim Girls' School in Post-riot Ahmedabad', in Meenakshi Thapan, ed., *Ethnographies of Schooling in Contemporary India* (New Delhi: Sage, 2014), pp. 228–29.

13. This section draws on authors' analysis of National Sample Survey (NSS) data on education and NSS data on employment and unemployment.

14. Excluding Muslim OBCs.

15. Azra Razzack, 'Schooling and the Intra-world of Muslim Community', *Economic and Political Weekly* 54.4 (26 January 2019).

16. 'Nai Manzil' and '3Ts: Teachers, tiffin and toilet' are two other new schemes in this vein.

17. For a detailed analysis of the scheme, see the evaluation report submitted by the Dr K.R. Narayanan Centre for Dalit and Minorities Studies, Jamia Millia Islamia.

18. Dhamma Darshan Nigam, 'I, a Manual Scavenger, Not Your Vote Bank', *Economic and Political Weekly* (11 October 2014).

19. Sonalde Desai and Veena Kulkarni, 'Unequal Playing Field: Socio-religious Inequalities in Educational Attainment', in Rakesh Basant and Abusaleh Shariff, *Handbook of Muslims in India: Empirical and Policy Perspectives* (New Delhi: Oxford University Press, 2010), p. 273.

20. Ibid, p. 274.

About the Contributors

Flavia Agnes is a feminist legal scholar and a women's rights lawyer. A pioneer of the women's movement, she has worked consistently on issues of violence against women. Her widely published writings have provided a vital context for feminist jurisprudence, human rights law and gender studies in India. Significant among her many publications are *Law & Gender Inequality: The Politics of Personal Laws in India* (1999), *Women and Law* (co-editor, 2004), *Family Law* (two volumes), a prescribed textbook for law students (2011), and *Negotiating Spaces* (co-editor, 2012). Agnes is a prominent advocate of legal pluralism. Her writings on this issue have provided a complex framework for protecting the rights of minority women within the rubric of legal pluralism.

Mahtab Alam is a multilingual journalist, writer and podcaster. His areas of interest include politics, law, literature, media and human rights. Currently, he is the executive editor of the Wire Urdu.

Amir Ali teaches at the Centre for Political Studies, Jawaharlal Nehru University, New Delhi. Previously, he taught at the department of political science, Jamia Millia Islamia, New Delhi and was Agatha Harrison Memorial visiting fellow at St Antony's College, Oxford. He is the author of *South Asian Islam and British Multiculturalism* (Routledge, 2016).

Muzna F. Alvi is an associate research fellow at the International Food Policy Research Institute. Her research interests include studying the relationship between ethnic and social identity and its effects on economic, educational and employment outcomes, particularly for women. Alvi has a PhD and an MA in economics from Michigan State University and an MPhil in economics from Jawaharlal Nehru University. She has previously worked with the World Bank and the Planning Commission of India.

Ankur Datta teaches sociology at the South Asian University, New Delhi. He is interested in the anthropology of violence, suffering and displacement, and the politics of victimhood in particular. He has conducted field work in Jammu and Kashmir. His work has been published in journals such as *Contributions to Indian Sociology*, *Modern Asian Studies* and *History and Anthropology*. He is the author of *On Uncertain Ground: Displaced Kashmiri Pandits in Jammu and Kashmir* (Oxford University Press, 2017).

Barbara Harriss–White is emeritus professor and fellow of Wolfson College, Oxford University, and visiting professor at JNU. Since 1969, she has worked on field economics research: on rural markets, development and policies affecting Indian agriculture, commodity markets, the informal economy and small towns. This work culminated in *India Working* (2003) in which she studied the relations between religions and the economy; *Middle India* (2015); and *The Wild East* (open access, 2019). She has also studied many aspects of deprivation and their relation to markets. After retirement, she has been researching markets for natural resources and waste. She has co-authored and edited forty books, and 265 papers and chapters.

Farah Naqvi is a feminist, writer and activist. She has worked on gender, caste and minority rights for over thirty years—from remote villages to public policy spaces. She was a member of the National Advisory Council (2010–14), Post-Sachar Evaluation Committee (Kundu Committee, 2013–14), Planning Commission Steering Committee (PCSC) on Empowerment of Minorities (2011–2012), PCSC for Women and Child Development (2007–08). She has authored two books: *Waves in the Hinterland* (2007), about Dalit women journalists, and *Working with Muslims: Beyond Burqa and Triple Talaq* (2017), about the voluntary sector's engagement with India's largest minority. She has worked extensively on targeted violence and justice; and is the co-director of *The Colour of My Home* (2018), a film set in post-2013 Muzaffarnagar about displacement, memory and the meaning of home.

Azra Razzack is a professor at the Dr K.R. Narayanan Centre for Dalit and Minorities Studies, Jamia Millia Islamia, New Delhi. Her research interests include the study of the marginalized, with a special focus on Muslims in India. Azra has earlier taught at the department of education, University of Delhi and was also a consultant with the Sachar Committee (2005–06).

Manisha Sethi teaches at Jamia Millia Islamia, New Delhi. She has written extensively on the discourse of counterterrorism and the legal regimes that accompany it, and her current work examines the relationship between religion and law. She is the author of *Escaping the World: Women Renouncers among Jains* (Routledge, 2012) and *Kafkaland: Law, Prejudice and Counterterrorism in India* (Three Essays Collective, 2014).

Navsharan Singh is a women's rights and human rights researcher and activist. Her involvement in the women's and democratic rights movement in India goes back a long time. Her academic and research interests include understanding mass sexual violence, impunity for systematic and widespread violations of human rights in several regions of India, Partition studies, labour rights, and Dalit land rights in Punjab. She also writes in Punjabi, and her writings have enabled her to address different audiences and engage in a range of debates in India. Navsharan has a PhD in political economy. She has co-edited *Landscapes of Fear: Understanding Impunity in India* (Zubaan, 2014).

About Samruddha Bharat Foundation

Samruddha Bharat Foundation is an independent socio-political organization established after the Dr B.R. Ambedkar International Conference held in July 2017 to:

1. Further India's constitutional promise
2. Forge an alliance of progressive forces
3. Encourage a transformative spirit in Indian politics and society.

Addressing both the symbolic and the substantive, SBF works to shape the polity, serve as a platform for participatory democracy, shape public discourse and deepen engagement with the diaspora.

In doing so, SBF works closely with India's major secular political parties on normative and policy issues. It has also created a praxis between India's foremost academics, activists and policymakers, as well as people's movements, civil society organizations, think tanks and institutions. Finally, it has established Bridge India as a sister organization in the United Kingdom to do similar work with the diaspora.

For further details, see:

www.samruddhabharat.in

 @SBFIndia

 Samruddha Bharat Foundation

 @SBFIndia